GREAT AMERICAN STORIES 1

1

Third Edition

Longman

C.G. Draper

Great American Stories 1: An ESL/EFL Reader

Third Edition

Pearson Education, 10 Bank Street, White Plains, NY 10606

Vice president, director of publishing: Allen Ascher
Editorial director: Louisa Hellegers
Acquisitions editor: Laura Le Dréan
Senior development manager: Penny Laporte
Development editor: Janet Johnston
Vice president, director of design and production: Rhea Banker
Executive managing editor: Linda Moser
Associate production editor: Melissa Leyva
Production supervisor: Ray Keating
Senior manufacturing buyer: Dave Dickey
Cover design: Elizabeth Carlson
Text design: Jill Yutkowitz
Text composition: Rainbow Graphics
Text art: Charles Shaw
Text credit: **Page 39:** "The Journey to Hanford" from MY NAME IS ARAM,
    copyright 1938 and renewed 1966 by William Saroyan, reprinted by permission
    of Harcourt, Inc.
Cover image: Tom Herzberg/Spots on the Spot/images.com

Library of Congress Cataloging-in-Publication Data

Draper, C.G.
    Great American stories 1: beginning-intermediate to intermediate levels/C.G.
    Draper.—3rd ed.
        p. cm.
    ISBN 0-13-030967-2 (alk. paper)
        1. English language—Textbooks for foreign speakers. 2. Short stories,
    American—Adaptations. 3. Readers—United States. I. Title.
PE1128 .D675 2001
428.6'4—dc21

                                                                    00-062328

ISBN: 0-13-030967-2

        7 8 9 10–CW–05 04

CONTENTS

TO THE TEACHER

GREAT AMERICAN STORIES 1 third edition consists of nine careful adaptations of famous stories by classic American writers and exercises on each story in reading skills, vocabulary, discussion, word forms, language activity, and writing. Prereading exercises introduce the student to the world of the story; one of the prereading exercises in each lesson is based on the biographical paragraph about the story's author that appears on the story's title page. Three new stories have been added to this edition, and two were dropped from the previous edition. A new Key Words section introduces the students to the words that are central to their understanding of the story. Word form charts have been added to many of the chapters, to help students master word families. In addition, a majority of the exercises have been revised and expanded based on teacher feedback.

The book is both graded and progressive—that is, the vocabulary, grammar, and internal structure of the stories increase in difficulty from the first story (which is at the beginning-intermediate level of proficiency) to the last (which is at the intermediate level). Structural, lexical, and sentence-length controls have been used throughout the book. The head-word list for the first five stories contains 600 words, while that used for the final four contains 1,000. Maximum sentence length increases from 10 words in the first story to 20 in the final four. New grammatical structures are added gradually, story by story, and words from outside the head-word lists are introduced in a context that makes their meanings clear, are used again within the next 100 words of text, and then are repeated at least three more times before the end of the story.

The exercises are designed so that the student must return to the text often to check comprehension or vocabulary. In addition, skimming and scanning exercises in the prereading sections may involve rereading of the writers' biographies. In short, an objective of the book is to involve the reader deeply in the text of each story and the world of its author, and, toward that end, to present exercises that are difficult if not impossible to complete without a thorough understanding of the text.

Finally, the book is designed for use either in or out of class—as a core reading text or ancillary text, or simply for pleasure reading. Its in-class use can take a number of different forms: teacher–student, student–student (pairs or small groups), student alone, or student–tutor.

C.G.D.

TO THE READER

This book begins at the beginning-intermediate level. It ends at the intermediate level. The first story in the book will be easy for you. The vocabulary list for the first five stories has 600 words. The list for the last five stories has 1,000 words. The longest sentences in the first story have 10 words. In the later stories, they have 20 words. There is new grammar in each story.

By using this book, you will improve your reading, speaking and discussion, vocabulary, knowledge of word forms, and writing.

These stories were written many years ago by nine of America's most famous writers. You will read about the writers' lives before you read their stories. Special exercises will introduce you to the world of each story before you read it. And after each story you will find 2 reading exercises, 2 vocabulary and word form exercises, 2 discussion and language activity exercises, and 1 writing exercise.

C.D.G.

THE GIFT OF THE MAGI

Adapted from the story by
O. HENRY

O. Henry's real name was William Sydney Porter. He was born in Greensboro, North Carolina, in 1862. He left school at the age of fifteen and worked in many different places. He also spent three years in prison because he took money from a bank. He started to write stories while he was in prison. O. Henry is famous for his stories with surprise endings. "The Gift of the Magi" is his most famous story. It is from the book *The Four Million,* stories about the everyday people of New York City. O. Henry died in 1910.

BEFORE YOU READ THE STORY

A. About the Author

Read the paragraph about O. Henry on page 1. What do you think is the most interesting thing about O. Henry's life?

B. Scanning for Information

Reading quickly to find small pieces of information is called *scanning*. First read the questions below. The answer to each question is in the paragraph about O. Henry on page 1. Then read the paragraph quickly, looking only for the information that will answer each question. Try to find each answer in thirty seconds or less.

1. In what town was O. Henry born?
2. How old was he when he left school?
3. Why did he go to prison?
4. What is O. Henry famous for?
5. What is *The Four Million*?
6. How old was O. Henry when he died?

C. The Pictures

1. Look at the pictures on page 4 and page 7. The same woman is in both pictures. Look at her face, her hair, and her clothes. What is the same? What is different?
2. Look at the picture of the three kings on page 6. Do you know who they were? Each king is carrying a gift. What do you think these gifts are?

D. Thinking About It

"The Gift of the Magi" happens at Christmas (December 25). In many countries, people give gifts at this time of year. When do you give gifts? Why do you give gifts?

comb   People usually *comb* their hair in the morning. If they don't have a *comb*, they might use their fingers. Women with long hair sometimes put special *combs* in their hair. The *combs* hold up their hair and add beauty.

Magi   The word *Magi* (MAY-jai) means "wise men." The three kings on page 6 are the *Magi*. They are carrying gifts for the baby Jesus.

watch and chain   A *watch* tells us the time. Usually, we wear a *watch* on our wrist (lower arm). Many years ago, men carried their *watches* in the pockets of their clothes. This kind of *watch* was often at the end of a special *chain* for *watches*. In the picture on page 7, the man is holding one of these *watch chains*.

THE GIFT OF THE MAGI

Della counted her money three times. She had only one dollar and eighty-seven cents. That was all. And tomorrow would be Christmas. What Christmas gift could she buy with only one dollar and eighty-seven cents? Della lay down on the old bed and cried and cried.

2   Let's leave Della alone for a while and look at her home. The chairs and tables were old and poor. Outside there was a mailbox without mail, and a door without a doorbell. The name on the door said Mr. JAMES DILLING-HAM YOUNG—Della's dear husband, Jim.

3   Della knew that Jim would be home soon. She dried her eyes and stood up. She looked in the mirror. She began to comb her hair for Jim. She felt very sad. She wanted to buy Jim a Christmas gift—something good. But what could she do with one dollar and eighty-seven cents? She combed her hair in front of the mirror and thought. Suddenly she had an idea.

4   Now, Jim and Della had only two treasures. One was Jim's gold watch. The other was Della's hair. It was long and

brown, and fell down her back. Della looked in the mirror a little longer. Her eyes were sad, but then she smiled. She put on her old brown coat and her hat. She ran out of the house and down the street. She stopped in front of a door which said, MME. SOPHRONIE. HAIR OF ALL KINDS. Madame Sophronie was fat and seemed too white. The store was dark.

5   "Will you buy my hair?" Della asked.

6   "I buy hair," said Madame. "Take off your hat. Let's see your hair."

7   Della took off her hat. Her hair fell down like water. Mme. Sophronie lifted Della's hair with a heavy hand. "Twenty dollars," she said.

8   "Give me the money now!" said Della.

9   Ah! the next two hours flew past like summer wind. Della shopped in many stores for the right gift for Jim. Then she found it—a chain for his gold watch. It was a good chain, strong and expensive. Della knew the chain would make Jim happy. Jim had a cheap chain for his watch, but this chain was much better. It would look good with the gold watch. The chain cost twenty-one dollars. Della paid for the chain and ran home with eighty-seven cents.

10   At seven o'clock Della made coffee and started to cook dinner. Jim would be home soon. He was never late. Della heard Jim outside. She looked in the mirror again. "Oh! I hope Jim doesn't kill me!" Della smiled, but her eyes were wet. "But what could I do with only one dollar and eighty-seven cents?"

11   The door opened, and Jim came in and shut it. His face was thin and quiet. His coat was old, and he had no hat. He was only twenty-two. Jim stood still and looked at Della. He didn't speak. His eyes were strange. Della suddenly felt afraid. She did not understand him. She began to talk very fast. "Oh, Jim, dear, why do you look so strange? Don't look at me like that. I cut my hair and sold it. I wanted to buy you a Christmas gift. It will grow again—don't be angry. My hair grows very fast. Say 'Merry Christmas,' dear, and let's be happy. You don't know what I've got for you— it's beautiful."

12   "You cut your hair?" Jim spoke slowly.

13   "I cut it and sold it," Della answered. "Don't you like me now? I'm still me, aren't I?"

14   "You say that your hair is gone?" Jim asked again.

15   "Don't look for it, it's gone," Della said. "Be good to me, because it's Christmas. Shall we have dinner now, Jim?"

16   Jim seemed to wake up. He smiled. He took Della in his arms.

17   Let's leave them together for a while. They are happy, rich or poor. Do you know about the Magi? The Magi were wise men who brought Christmas gifts to the baby Jesus. But they could not give gifts like Jim's and Della's. Perhaps you don't understand me now. But you will understand soon.

18   Jim took a small box out of his pocket. "I love your short hair, Della," he said. "I'm sorry I seemed strange. But if you open the box, you will understand." Della opened the box. First she smiled, then suddenly she began to cry. In the box were two beautiful combs. Combs like those were made to hold up long hair. Della could see that the combs came from an expensive store. She never thought she would ever

have anything as beautiful! "Oh, Jim, they are lovely! And my hair grows fast, you know. But wait! You must see your gift." Della gave Jim the chain. The chain was bright, like her eyes. "Isn't it a good one, Jim? I looked for it everywhere. You'll have to look at the time one hundred times daily, now. Give me your watch. I want to see them together."

19 Jim lay back on the bed. He put his hands under his head, and smiled. "Della," he said, "let's put the gifts away. They are too good for us right now. I sold the watch to buy your combs. Come on, let's have dinner."

20 The Magi, as we said, were wise men—very wise men. They brought gifts to the baby Jesus. The Magi were wise, so their gifts were wise gifts. Perhaps Jim and Della do not seem wise. They lost the two great treasures of their house. But I want to tell you that they *were* wise. People like Jim and Della are always wiser than others. Everywhere they are wiser. They are the magi.

AFTER YOU READ THE STORY

A. Understanding the Main Ideas

Answer these questions with complete sentences.

1. Why did Della want to buy a gift for Jim?
2. Were Della and Jim rich? How do you know?
3. What were Jim's and Della's greatest treasures?
4. How did Della get enough money for Jim's gift?
5. How did Jim get enough money for Della's gift?
6. Who were the Magi, and what did they do?
7. Why does the writer think Della and Jim were wise?

B. Close Reading

If the sentence is true, write **T** next to it. If it is not true, write **F** for false. Then change one word to make it true.

_____ 1. Della and Jim were very poor.

_____ 2. Della was very happy before she bought Jim's present.

_____ 3. Madame Sophronie gave Della two dollars for her hair.

_____ 4. Before Christmas, Jim had an expensive chain for his watch.

_____ 5. Jim was young, but his coat was old.

_____ 6. Della laughed when Jim gave her the combs.

_____ 7. Jim didn't show Della his watch.

C. Discussion

1. The writer, O. Henry, tells us that the Magi were wise. He also says that Jim and Della were wise. Why does he say this? Were they all wise in the same way? Do you agree with O. Henry?
2. A gift is one way of showing love. Do you think it is a very important way? Why, or why not?
3. Do you give gifts to everyone you love? Do you ever give gifts to people you don't love? If so, why? If not, why not?

D. Vocabulary Practice

For each space in the sentences below, choose the best word from the following list.

mirror	watch	gift	wise
count	treasures	doorbell	comb

1. Della needed to _____ her money many times.

2. Della's hair and Jim's watch were their two great

   _____.

3. When Della looked in the _____, she saw her long

   hair.

4. Della's _____ to Jim was a chain for his watch.

5. Jim gave Della not just one beautiful _____ for her

   hair, but two of them.

6. At the beginning of the story, Jim has a cheap chain for his

   _____. At the end, he has an expensive chain.

7. Jim and Della's door had no _____.

8. Were Jim and Della _____ to give the gift of love?

E. Word Forms

A *noun* is a person, place, or thing. An *adjective* describes a person, place, or thing. Write the noun form in its correct space. Write the adjective form in its correct space.

1. (*sad / sadness*) Della's _____ came from not having

   enough money to buy Jim a present. But she was not

   _____ to lose the great treasure of her hair. Why?

2. (*wise / wisdom*) People say that great _____ comes

   with old age. Do the Magi on page 6 look _____?

   Do they look old?

3. (*happy / happiness*) Della was _____ to see Jim's

   beautiful gift. But her greatest _____ came from

   giving a gift to Jim.

4. (*heavy / heaviness*) The _____ of Della's hair

   surprised Madame Sophronie. "With hair this

   _____," she thought, "I will make a lot of

   money."

5. (*expensive / expense*) The _____ of a good watch

   chain was too great for Jim. But at the end of the story he

   had an _____ watch chain. And no watch!

F. Language Activity: An Interview

Write your answers to these questions.

1. What is your greatest treasure?
2. When did you get it?
3. How did you get it?
4. Why is it such a treasure to you?
5. Would you ever sell it?
6. Would you ever give it away?

Choose a partner from class who has also answered the questions. Discuss your answers together. Then tell the class what you learned from those answers.

G. Writing: Madame Sophronie Speaks

In this exercise, you are Madame Sophronie. Answer each question in complete sentences. The information in paragraphs 4–7 will help you.

Example:

What is your name? Do you have a store in the city, or in the country?

My name is Madame Sophronie. I have a store in the city.

1. Do you buy and sell hair, or do you buy and sell gold chains?
2. One day, did a young woman come into your store, or was it her husband?
3. Did she want to sell her hair, or buy it?
4. Did you tell her to take her hat off, or to put it on?
5. Did she have beautiful long hair, or beautiful short hair?
6. How much did you pay for it?
7. Did you plan to sell it later for more money, or for less money?

After you have answered the seven questions, put your answers together in one paragraph. Begin the paragraph with the sentences **My name is Madame Sophronie. I have a store in the city.**

Now, add a second paragraph with your answers to the following questions. You will find the answers to these questions in your mind, not in the story.

1. The next day, did a rich woman or a poor woman come into your store?
2. Did she like the young woman's hair a lot, or just a little?
3. How much did you ask her to pay for it?
4. How much did she want to pay for it?
5. In the end, how much did she pay for it?
6. Did you feel happy, sad, or just OK about that price?

2

LOVE OF LIFE

Adapted from the story by
JACK LONDON

Jack London was born in San Francisco, in 1876. His family was poor. He left school at fourteen. He worked on boats, on farms, and in the woods. He loved to visit new places. His first long trip was to Japan. When he was eighteen he returned to high school for one year. Then he went to the University of California at Berkeley. But again he left after one year and began to write for money. In 1897 he went to the Klondike, in northwest Canada, near Alaska. Many men went to find gold in that cold, empty land. London wrote stories about the men and animals there. He traveled to many other different places, too, and found adventures everywhere. He put these adventures into his famous stories and novels. London continued to travel until a few years before his death in 1916.

BEFORE YOU READ THE STORY

A. About the Author

1. Read the paragraph about Jack London on page 13. Why do you think London wrote adventure stories?
2. The paragraph tells us that London went to the Klondike in 1897. Where is the Klondike? Why did men go there at that time? What kind of place was it?

B. The Pictures

Look closely at the pictures on pages 16, 18, 20, and 21. Without reading the story, try to answer the questions below. Do this exercise with a classmate, and report your answers to the class.

1. In the first picture, is one man walking away from the other, or toward him? What is the man in the water carrying? Describe the land around the two men.
2. In the picture on page 18, animal bones are on the ground. Why do you think the man is reaching for the bones?
3. In the picture on page 21, do you think the animal (a wolf) is friendly? Is the man in the picture sleeping, or dead?

C. Thinking About It

Tell your own story about the man in the four pictures. Use all four pictures in your story.

D. Skimming

Sometimes we want a general idea about a piece of writing before we read it carefully. Fast reading for the general idea is called *skimming*. This exercise will show you one way of skimming.

Read the first two sentences of each paragraph in "Love of Life." Take one minute (sixty seconds) to do this. Next, answer these questions. Do not look back at the story to answer them.

1. How many men are in the story at the beginning?
2. Does the man hurt his foot, or his hand?
3. Is the man hungry, or thirsty? Is he warm, or cold? Is he sick, or well?
4. Who finally finds the man? Is he alive, or is he dead?

blanket   A *blanket* is a large, heavy cloth. You put a *blanket* on your bed or around your shoulders when you are cold.

bullets   *Bullets* are shot out of a gun.

camp   A *camp* is a place to live in a field or in the woods. A *camp* can be a simple building or just a tent. You feel less cold and less danger in a *camp* than in the open. You can leave blankets, bullets, and food in your *camp* and go back to them later.

hunger   *Hunger* is a strong need to eat.

wolf   The animal in the picture on page 21 is a *wolf*.

LOVE OF LIFE

Two men walked slowly through the low water of a river. They were alone in the cold, empty land. All they could see were stones and earth. It was fall, and the river ran cold over their feet. They carried blankets on their backs. They had guns, but no bullets; matches, but no food.

2   "I wish we had just two of those bullets we hid in the camp," said the first of the men. His voice was tired. The other man did not answer.

3   Suddenly the first man fell over a stone. He hurt his foot badly, and he cried out. He lay still for a moment, and then called: "Hey, Bill, I've hurt my foot." Bill didn't stop or look back. He walked out of the river and over the hill. The other man watched him. His eyes seemed like the eyes of a sick animal. He stood up. "Bill!" he cried again. But there was no answer. Bill kept walking.

4   "Bill!"

5   The man was alone in the empty land. His hands were cold, and he dropped his gun. He fought with his fear, and took his gun out of the water. He followed slowly after Bill. He tried to walk lightly on his bad foot.

6   He was alone, but he was not lost. He knew the way to their camp. There he would find food, bullets, and blankets. He must find them soon. Bill would wait for him there. Together they would go south to the Hudson Bay Company. They would find food there, and a warm fire. Home. The man had to believe that Bill would wait for him at the camp. If not, he would die. He thought about the food in the camp. And the food at the Hudson Bay Company. And the food he ate two days ago. He thought about food and he walked. After a while the man found some small berries to eat. The berries had no taste, and did not fill him. But he knew he must eat them.

7   In the evening he hit his foot on a stone and fell down. He could not get up again. He lay still for a long time. Later, he felt a little better and got up. He made a fire. He could cook only hot water, but he felt warmer. He dried his shoes by the fire. They had many holes. His feet had blood on them. His foot hurt badly. He put his foot in a piece of his blanket. Then he slept like a dead man.

8   He woke up because he heard an animal near him. He thought of meat and took his gun. But he had no bullets. The animal ran away. The man stood up and cried out. His foot was much worse this morning. He took out a small bag that was in his blanket. It was heavy—fifteen pounds. He didn't know if he could carry it. But he couldn't leave it behind. He had to take it with him. He had to be strong enough. He put it into his blanket again.

9   That day his hunger grew worse, worse than the hurt in his foot. Many times he wanted to lie down, but hunger made him go on. He saw a few birds. Once he tried to catch one, but it flew away. He felt tired and sick. He forgot to follow the way to the camp. In the afternoon he found some green plants. He ate them fast, like a horse. He saw a small fish in a river. He tried to catch it with his cup. But the fish swam away into a hole. The man cried like a baby, first quietly, then loudly. He cried alone in that empty world.

10   That night he made a fire again, and drank hot water. His blanket was wet, and his foot hurt. He could think only of his hunger. He woke up cold and sick. The earth and sky were gray. He got up and walked, he didn't know where. But the small bag was with him. The sun came out again, and he saw that he was lost. Was he too far north? He

turned toward the east. His hunger was not so great, but he knew he was sick. He stopped often. He heard wolves, and knew that deer were near him. He believed he had one more bullet in his gun. But it was still empty. The small bag became too heavy. The man opened the bag. It was full of small pieces of gold. He put half the gold in a piece of his blanket and left it on a rock. But he kept his gun. There were bullets in that camp.

11   Days passed, days of rain and cold. One day he came to the bones of a deer. There was no meat on the bones. The man knew wolves must be near. He broke the bones and ate like an animal. Would he, too, be only bones tomorrow? And why not? This was life, he thought. Only life hurt. There was no hurt in death. To die was to sleep. Then why was he not ready to die? He could not see or feel. The hunger, too, was gone. But he walked and walked.

12   One morning he woke up beside a river. Sunlight was warm on his face. A sunny day, he thought. Perhaps he could find his way to the camp. His eyes followed the river. He could see far. The river emptied into the sea. He saw a ship on that silver sea. He shut his eyes. He knew there could be no ship, no seas, in this land. He heard a noise behind him, and turned back. A wolf, old and sick, was following him. I know *this* is real, he thought. He turned again, but the sea and the ship were still there. He didn't understand it. He tried to remember. What did the men at the Hudson Bay Company say about this land? Was he walking north, away from the camp, toward the sea? The man moved slowly toward the ship. He knew the sick wolf was following him. In the afternoon, he found more bones left by wolves. The bones of a man! Beside the bones was a small bag of gold, like his own. Ha! Bill carried his gold to the end, he thought. He would take Bill's gold to the ship. He would have the last laugh on Bill. His laughing sounded like the low cry of an animal. The wolf cried back to the man, and the man stopped laughing. How could he laugh about Bill's bones? He could not take Bill's gold. He left the gold near the bones.

13   The man was very sick now. He walked more and more slowly. His blanket was gone. He lost his gold, then his gun, then his knife. Only the wolf stayed with him hour after hour. At last the man could go no further. He fell down. The

wolf came close to him. It weakly bit his hand. The man hit the wolf and it went away. But it did not go far. It waited. The man waited. After many hours the wolf came back again. It was going to kill the man. But the man was ready. He held the wolf's mouth closed, and he got on top of the sick wolf. He held the animal still. Then he bit it with his last strength. He tasted the wolf's blood in his mouth. Only love of life gave him enough strength. He held the wolf with his teeth and killed it. Later he fell on his back and slept.

14   The men on the ship saw a strange thing on the land. It did not walk. It was lying on the ground, and it moved slowly toward them—perhaps twenty feet an hour. The men went close to look at it. They could not believe it was a man.

15   Three weeks later the man felt better. He could tell them his story. But there was one strange thing. He could not believe there was enough food on the ship. The men told him there was a lot of food. But he only looked at them with fear. And slowly he began to grow fat. The men thought this was strange. They gave him less food, but still he grew larger and larger—each day he was fatter. Then one day they saw him put a lot of bread under his shirt. They looked in his bed, too, and saw bread under his blanket. The men understood, and left him alone.

AFTER YOU READ THE STORY

A. Understanding the Main Ideas

Read these sentences from the story. Then answer the questions about the sentences.

1. "*Bill didn't stop or look back.*" (paragraph 3)
   Who was Bill? Why do you think he didn't stop or look back?

2. "*He took out a small bag that was in his blanket.*" (paragraph 8)
   What was in this bag? (paragraph 10) Did the man keep it, or lose it? (paragraph 13) Why?

3. "*. . . the fish swam away into a hole. The man cried like a baby, first quietly, then loudly.*" (paragraph 9)
   Why did the man cry about losing the fish?

4. "*He saw a ship on that silver sea.*" (paragraph 12)
   Did he think the ship was real? Why, or why not? Was the ship real?

5. "*But he only looked at them with fear.*" (paragraph 15)
   Was the man safe on the ship? Did he have enough food to eat? Why was he still afraid?

6. "Love of Life" is the title of the story. What does it mean? How does the man show that he loves life?

B. Close Reading

Choose the correct word to complete each sentence.

1. The man could not walk quickly because he hurt his _____ .

   a. back   **b.** foot   **c.** hand

2. The man wanted to find the camp because of the _____ there.

   a. gold   **b.** water   **c.** bullets and food

3. One day the man found and ate the bones of a _____ .

   a. deer   **b.** fish   **c.** wolf

4. The wolf could not kill the man because the wolf, too, was
_____ .

    a. hungry   **b.** thirsty   **c.** weak

5. The man found Bill's _____ .

    a. hat and gloves **b.** bones and gold **c.** blanket and bullets

6. The men on the ship did not take the man's hidden _____ .

    a. meat   **b.** blanket   **c.** bread

7. The men on the ship understood why the man was always
_____ .

    a. hungry   **b.** angry   **c.** laughing

C. Vocabulary Practice

An *antonym* is a word that means the opposite of another word.
Good and *bad* are antonyms. *Big* and *little* are antonyms. Find
the antonym in column A for each word in column B. Write the
number. The first one is done for you.

A		**B**
1. weak	_____	life
2. lost	_____	open
3. laugh	_____	full
4. death	_____	thin
5. follow	_____	cry
6. empty	_____	loudly
7. quietly	_1_	strong
8. closed	_____	found
9. fat	_____	lead

D. Discussion

1. When the man finds Bill's gold, why does he laugh? Why
does he stop laughing? Why does he leave the gold where he
found it?

2. "Empty" land has almost no people on it. Do you know land that is "empty"? Where is it? Describe it. Have you ever walked there? Did you like it? Would you like to live there?

E. Word Forms

Adverbs tell us <u>how</u> something happens. *Adverbs* are usually made by adding the letters *-ly* to the *adjective* form. Write the adjective form in its correct space. Write the adverb form in its correct space.

1. (*slow / slowly*) The man walked very _____. But the sick wolf was _____, too.

2. (*sudden / suddenly*) Bill had a _____ thought: "If I die _____, what will happen to my gold?"

3. (*tired / tiredly*) The man was hungry and _____. When he walked _____ onto the ship, the men there watched him without speaking.

4. (*weak / weakly*) The wolf was _____, like the man, and could only bite him _____.

5. (*hungry / hungrily*) The man ate the bones _____, like an animal. He was so _____ he could think only of food.

F. Language Activity: Riddles

Choose a word from the list that fits each sentence. The first one is done for you.

a. bag	**c.** blanket	**e.** hunger	**g.** camp
b. strength	**d.** bullet	**f.** wolf	**h.** bones

1. __d__ Without this little thing, he could not use the big thing he carried with him.

2. _____ He made pieces of it—one for his hurt foot, one for his gold.

3. _____ He killed it the way it wanted to kill him.

4. _____ He ate them, and he thought he might die and become them.

5. _____ He didn't want it, but every day he had more of it.

6. _____ He needed it, but every day he had less of it.

7. _____ It had everything he wanted, but he couldn't find it.

8. _____ He carried his gold in it.

G. Writing: The Captain Writes a Letter Home

You are the captain of the ship in "Love of Life." You are writing a letter to your wife. Your letter begins:

My dear Ellen,

I'm sorry I can't send you letters more often. We come to land only once a month. Last month, something very strange happened. I want to tell you about it.

We were on the sea. I saw something very strange on the land, and I decided to look closely at it.

Continue your letter by answering the questions below. Use complete sentences. When two questions are together, join your answers using the word in parentheses. The information in paragraphs 14 and 15 can help you answer the questions.

Example:

Did you see something very strange on the land, or in the water? Did you decide to look closely at it, or to run away? (*and*)

I saw something very strange on the land, and I decided to look closely at it.

1. Was it lying on the ground, or standing up? Was it moving very slowly, or very quickly? (*and*)

2. Did you think it was an animal, or a rock? Was it a man, or a wolf? (*but*)

3. On the ship, little by little, did the man get stronger, or weaker?

4. Did he eat a lot of food, or no food? Did he look at the other men with fear, or with happiness? (*but*)

5. Could he believe there was enough food on the ship, or not?

6. One day, did the men see him hide bread, or throw bread away? Did they stop him, or not? (*but*)
7. Did the men understand, or did they laugh at him? Did they leave him alone, or did they throw him in the sea? (*and*)

Your letter ends:

So you see, my dear Ellen, strange things happen in this world. I feel very alone without you, and I hope to see you soon. Kiss the children for me.

Your loving husband,
Captain Jack

3

THE STORY OF AN HOUR

Adapted from the story by

KATE CHOPIN

Kate Chopin was born in 1851 in St. Louis, Missouri. Her family was rich. She married, and had six children. She lived a family life like other rich ladies in those days. But she was well educated and liked to read and write. After her husband died in 1883, she began to write stories. She also wrote a book called *The Awakening*. This book, and many of her stories, shocked her readers at that time. She wrote about the freedom of women. But at that time, most women lived only for their families. Because the stories were shocking, people did not read them for many years after her death in 1904. Now Kate Chopin's writing has been discovered again. People are interested in her life and work.

BEFORE YOU READ THE STORY

A. About the Author

Read the paragraph about Kate Chopin on page 27. The word *shocked* means "deeply surprised." The word *freedom* means "being free." What were many of Chopin's stories about? Why do you think they were almost forgotten for many years?

B. Scanning Two Different Sources of Information

For this exercise, use the paragraphs about Jack London, on page 13, and Kate Chopin, on page 27. Read each question below, then quickly scan the paragraphs about the two writers. Find the answer to the question. You do not need to find any other information. Try to do the exercise in three minutes or less.

1. Which writer was born earlier?
2. Which writer was born to a rich family?
3. Which writer started writing when young?
4. Which writer traveled a lot?
5. Which writer died later than the other?
6. Which writer died older than the other?

C. The Pictures

1. The same woman is in the pictures on page 30 and page 32. What is she feeling in the first picture? How has she changed in the second?
2. What do you think is happening in the picture on page 33?

D. Thinking About It

"The Story of an Hour" is about a marriage more than 100 years ago. Have marriages changed in the past 100 years? In what ways? In what ways have they not changed?

accident   The story opens with a train *accident*. A person can be killed in a bad *accident*. Yesterday my son had a little *accident*. He spilled a glass of milk on his pants. Then the *accident* got worse. He fell off the chair and hurt his arm.

broken   Watch me *break* this pencil in half. There! I *broke* it. Now the pencil is *broken*.

excitement   The girl was *excited* by her first ride on a horse. Her color, her bright eyes, and her laughter all showed her *excitement*.

freedom   He kept the bird in a box; it was not *free*. When he opened the box, he gave the bird its *freedom*, and it flew away.

joyful   He was very happy to have a daughter after two sons. The baby girl gave him great *joy*. When she smiled, her happy face was *joyful*, and his heart filled with *joy*.

THE STORY OF AN HOUR

They knew that Louise Mallard had a weak heart. So they broke the bad news softly. Her husband, Brently, was dead.

2   "There was a train accident, Louise," said her sister, Josephine, quietly.

3   Her husband's friend, Richards, stood with Josephine. Richards brought the news, but Josephine told the story. She spoke in broken sentences.

4   "Richards . . . was at the newspaper office. News of the accident came. Louise . . . Louise, Brently's name was on the list. Brently . . . was killed, Louise."

5   Louise did not hear the story coldly, like some women would. She could not close her mind or her heart to the news. Like a sudden storm, her tears broke out. She cried loudly in her sister's arms. Then, just as suddenly, the tears stopped. She went to her room alone. She wanted no one with her.

6   In front of the window stood an empty chair. She sat down and looked out the window. She was very tired after her tears. Her body felt cold, her mind and heart were empty.

7   Outside her window she could see the trees. The air smelled like spring rain. She could hear someone singing far away. Birds sang near the house. Blue sky showed between the clouds. She rested.

8   She sat quietly, but a few weak tears still fell. She had a young, strong face. But now her eyes showed nothing. She looked out the window at the blue sky. She was not thinking, or seeing. She was waiting.

9   There was something coming to her. She was waiting for it with fear. What was it? She did not know; she could not give it a name. But she felt it coming out from the sky. It reached her through the sound, the smell, the color of the air.

10   Slowly she became excited. Her breath came fast, her heart beat faster. She began to see this thing. It wanted to find her and take her. She tried to fight against it. But she could not. Her mind was as weak as her two small white hands. Then she stopped fighting against it. A little word broke from her lips.

11   "Free," she said. "Free, free, free!" The emptiness and fear left her. Her eyes showed her excitement. Her heart beat fast, and the blood warmed her body. A sudden feeling of joy excited her.

12   She did not stop to ask if her joy was wrong. She saw her freedom clearly. She could not stop to think of smaller things.

13   She knew the tears would come again when she saw her husband's body. The kind hands, now dead and still. The loving face, now still and gray. But she looked into the future. She saw many long years to come that would belong to her alone. And now she opened her arms wide to those years in welcome.

14   There would be no one else to live for during those years. She would live for herself alone. There would be no strong mind above hers. Men and women always believe they can tell others what to do and how to think. Suddenly Louise understood that this was wrong. She could break away and be free of it.

15   And yet, she loved him—sometimes. Often she did not. What did love mean now? Now she understood that freedom is stronger than love.

16   "Free! Body and mind free!" she said again.

17   Her sister, Josephine, was waiting outside the door.

18   "Please open the door," Josephine cried. "You will make yourself sick. What are you doing in there, Louise? Please, please, let me in!"

19   "Go away. I am not sick." No, she was drinking in life through that open window.

20   She thought joyfully of all those days before her. Spring days, summer days. All kinds of days that would be her own. She began to hope life would be long. And just yesterday, life seemed too long!

21   After a while she got up and opened the door. Her eyes were bright, her cheeks were red. She didn't know how strong and well she looked—so full of joy. They went downstairs, where Richards was waiting.

22   A man was opening the door. It was Brently Mallard. He was dirty, and tired. He carried a suitcase and an umbrella. He was not killed in the train accident. He didn't even know there was an accident. He was surprised at Josephine's sudden cry. He didn't understand why Richards moved suddenly between them, to hide Louise from her husband.

23   But Richards was too late.

24   When the doctors came, they said it was her weak heart. They said she died of joy—of joy that kills.

AFTER YOU READ THE STORY

A. Understanding the Main Ideas

Answer these questions with complete sentences.

1. What news did Richards give Louise?
2. How did Louise act when she first heard the news?
3. What was Louise waiting for when she was alone in her room?
4. Why did her sadness change to joy?
5. When Brently came home, why was everyone surprised?
6. "They said she died of joy." Did she? If not, what did she die of?

B. Close Reading

Choose one of the two words in parentheses to make the correct sentence.

1. Louise Mallard had a (*cold* / *weak*) heart.
2. They said (*Brently* / *Richards*) was killed in a train accident.
3. Sitting near the window, Louise was waiting to understand (*her feelings* / *her husband*).
4. At first, Louise (*welcomed* / *fought against*) the strange feeling that came to her.
5. She understood that freedom is (*stronger* / *weaker*) than love.
6. She knew she could live her life (*with Josephine* / *alone*).
7. After her husband died, she hoped that her life would be (*short* / *long*).
8. Richards tried to hide Brently from (*Louise* / *Josephine*).

C. Discussion

1. Look at this sentence from paragraph 15: "*Now she understood that freedom is stronger than love.*" What do you think of this idea? Does it shock you? What kind of freedom did Louise find? Where did she find it? What kind of love was weaker than this freedom?
2. Louise thinks, "*Men and women always believe they can tell others what to do and how to think.*" (paragraph 14) Why do you think she believes this? Do you agree with her? How do people try to tell other people what to do and how to think?

3. What does Louise mean when she says, *"Free, free, free!"* (paragraph 11)? Free from what? Today, are women more free than men, or less free? Why? Are women freer in some countries than in others? Why?

D. Vocabulary Practice

Complete the sentences below in a way that shows the meaning of the underlined word. The number of the paragraph where the word appears is in parentheses.

Example:

It was a very bad <u>accident</u>. Two people <u>died when the car left the</u> <u>road and hit a tree.</u>

(paragraph 2)

1. My aunt was very <u>surprised</u> when _____

   _____ .

   (paragraph 22)

2. Do you know what was really <u>shocking</u> about that movie? It was _____

   _____ .

   (paragraph on Chopin's life, page 27)

3. How did the dog show his <u>excitement?</u> I'll tell you. It was funny. He _____

   _____ .

   (paragraph 11)

4. I felt that my heart was <u>broken</u> when _____

   _____ .

   (paragraph 3)

E. Word Forms

Below is a chart showing the parts of speech, or word forms, of some key words in the story. The chart will help you complete the exercise below.

Noun	Verb	Adjective	Adverb
freedom	free	free	freely
excitement	excite	excited, exciting	excitedly
break	break	broken	brokenly
surprise	surprise	surprised, surprising	surprisingly
joy		joyful	joyfully
understanding	understand	understanding	understandingly

Choose the correct form of the word in parentheses to complete the sentence.

Example:

(*surprise* / *surprising* / *surprisingly*) Brently's death was a <u>surprise</u> that made Louise very sad. But, <u>surprisingly,</u> her sadness changed to joy when she thought of her new freedom. Brently's <u>surprising</u> return home took away her freedom and her life.

1. (*broke* / *broken* / *brokenly*) Josephine spoke _____ to Louise about Brently's death. She cried, too, when Louise's tears _____ out. Josephine thought Louise's heart was _____.

2. (*understand* / *understanding* / *understandingly*) "Please open the door. You will make yourself sick!" Josephine said to her sister _____. But when Louise came out, Josephine couldn't _____ why she looked so strong and well. Josephine was not very _____ of Louise's mind and heart.

3. (*joy* / *joyful* / *joyfully*) The _____ that Louise felt surprised her. She spoke _____ to her sister, and lifted _____ eyes to Richards.

4. (*excitement / excited / excitedly*) Louise slowly became

_____ as a feeling of joy came to her. Her eyes

showed her _____. After a while she walked

_____ to the door and opened it.

5. (*free / freely / freedom*) Louise gave herself _____

to the strange, new, joyful feeling. Now _____ was

hers! Now her heart, body, and mind were _____!

F. Language Activity: The Role of Women

In the section "Before You Read the Story," Exercise D asked
you to think about the way marriages have changed in the past
100 years. Keeping those thoughts in mind, work with a partner
or small group from your class, if possible. Think of magazines,
newspapers, or television programs that show you something
about the role of women in today's world. What do the want ads
(job advertisements) tell you? What do advertisements for clothes
tell you? What do TV programs about families tell you? Find a
magazine or newspaper that is at least thirty years old. Or choose
an old movie or TV show that your partner or group has seen.
What do these things say about the role of women? Have
women's roles changed? How, and how much? Report to the
class on what you find. If you have a problem finding information, use what you know about your sisters, mothers, and grand-
mothers. Is the role of women different in different countries?

G. Writing: Josephine's Diary

You are Louise's sister, Josephine. Every day, you write in a
diary. You write what happened that day, and how you feel
about it. Here, you are writing about what happened on the day
Louise died. Complete each sentence in Josephine's diary with
your own words.

Dear Diary,

Our friend Richards brought the saddest news today. _____

_____

_____ .

After Louise heard about it, she _____

_____ .

Then she _____

_____ .

I was so worried about her! I called and called outside her
door, and _____

_____ .

I couldn't understand why she looked _____

_____ .

We went downstairs to see Richards. Suddenly, the door
opened, and Brently _____

_____ .

We couldn't understand what had happened. I _____ ,
Richards _____, and Louise _____ .
Later, the doctors _____ .
I don't know what Brently thought. But I think _____

_____ .

4

THE JOURNEY TO HANFORD

Adapted from the story by
WILLIAM SAROYAN

William Saroyan's family came to the United States from Armenia. His older brother and sisters were born there, and William was born in Fresno, California, in 1908. The Saroyan family was large and loving, but very poor. After Saroyan's father died when Saroyan was only three, his mother had no money at all. She had to put her children in an orphanage (a home for children with no parents) for five years. Saroyan began working at the age of eight, selling newspapers. He left school at the age of fourteen. He decided to become a writer, and taught himself by reading. He wrote stories, poems, and plays. His work is often about his own life and his own family. The story that follows, "A Journey to Hanford," is from the book *My Name Is Aram*. All the stories in this book are told by Aram, a boy in a large, poor Armenian family in the California farmlands. Saroyan writes about the goodness of people and the richness of life. He often writes about how people are able to find happiness, hope, and joy in very difficult times. Saroyan himself was not always happy with life in the United States. After 1958, he lived mostly in Paris. But he kept his home in Fresno, and he died there in 1981.

BEFORE YOU READ THE STORY

A. About the Author

Read the paragraph about William Saroyan on page 39. Write down three things you learned from this paragraph about Saroyan's early childhood.

B. The Pictures

1. Look at the picture on page 43. What family members could be in this picture? (Remember: my mother and father are my *parents*. My *grandfather* is the father of one of my parents. My *grandmother* is the mother of one of my parents. My *uncle* is the brother, and my *aunt* the sister, of one of my parents. My *cousins* are the children of my uncles and aunts.)
2. In the picture on page 47, the man outside the house is playing a *zither*, a stringed musical instrument. What is the man doing who is sitting on the chair inside the house?

C. Thinking About It

1. Did your parents, grandparents, or great-grandparents ever "change countries"? That is, did your family, sometime in the past, move from one country to another to live? From where to where?
2. Do you like living where you are now? If you could choose another place to live in, where would it be? Why?
3. Which do you like better: going to new places, or staying at home? Why?

D. Scanning

How fast can you find the following information from the paragraph about William Saroyan on page 39? Time yourself.

1. The year Saroyan was born: _____

   The year he died: _____

2. The place he was born: _____

   The place he died: _____

3. The name of a book of stories by Saroyan: _____

4. The place where he lived after 1958: _____

praise, perfect, punish   Son, if you do this job *perfectly*, without any mistakes, I will *praise* you with golden words. But if you do this job badly, I will *punish* you by keeping you at home every night this week.

rice, swill   In this story, a boy cooks *rice*—small white grains that he cooks in water. If he adds too much water, the *rice* will become like *swill*—that is, more like a bad soup than well-cooked grains. Real *swill* is made of leftover food mixed with water or bad milk, and fed to pigs.

season, watermelon   In this story, the time of year, or *season*, is summer. Summer is the *season* for *watermelon*—a large, round, heavy fruit, green on the outside, red on the inside, with many little black seeds in the red fruit.

tiger   A large, wild animal in the cat family

THE JOURNEY TO HANFORD

I

The time came one year for my sad uncle Jorgi to get on his bicycle and ride twenty-seven miles to Hanford. There was a job for him there in a farmer's field. Of course, before he went, the family had to decide who would go with him.

2   It is true that Jorgi was a kind of fool. That was all right with the family most of the time. But right now, in the summer, they wanted to forget him for a while. Now he would go away to Hanford and work in the watermelon fields. All would be well. He would earn a little money and at the same time be out of the way. That was the important thing—to get him out of the way.

3   "Away with him and his zither both," my grandfather said. "You will read in a book that a man can sit all day under a tree and play music on a zither and sing. Believe me, that writer is a fool. Money, that's the thing. Let him go and

work under the sun for a while. In the watermelons. Him and his zither both."

4   "You say that now," my grandmother said, "but wait a week. Wait, and you will need music again."

5   "Foolish words!" my grandfather said. "You will read in a book that a man who sings is truly a happy man. But that writer is a dreamer, not a businessman in a thousand years. Let him go. It is twenty-seven miles to Hanford. That is a very good distance."

6   "You speak that way *now*," my grandmother said. "But in three days you will be a sad man. I will see you walking around like a tiger. I will see you roar with anger. I am the one who will see that. Seeing that, I am the one who will laugh."

7   "You are a woman," said my grandfather. "You will read in a book that a woman is a perfect and beautiful thing. Believe me, that writer is not looking at his wife. He is dreaming."

8   "It is just that you are no longer young," my grandmother said. "That is why you are roaring."

9   "Close your mouth," my grandfather roared. "Close it right now!"

10   My grandfather looked around the room at his children and grandchildren. "I say he goes to Hanford on his bicycle," he said. "What do you say?"

11   Nobody spoke.

12   "Then it is done," my grandfather said. "Now, who shall we send with him on this journey? Which of our children shall we punish by sending him with Jorgi to Hanford? You will read in a book that a journey to a new city is a great thing for a young man. That writer is probably a fool of eighty or ninety. His only journey was two miles from home once when he was a little child. Who shall we punish? Vask? Shall Vask be the one? Step up here, boy."

13   My cousin Vask got up from the floor and stood in front of the old man. My grandfather put his hand over Vask's face. His hand almost covered the whole head.

14   "Shall you go with your uncle Jorgi to Hanford?" my grandfather said.

15   "If it pleases my grandfather, I will," Vask said.

16   The old man began to make faces, thinking about it.

17   "Let me think a minute," he said. "Jorgi is one of the foolish ones in our family. Vask is another. Is it wise to put two fools together? Let me hear your spoken thoughts on this."

18   "I think it is the right thing to do," my uncle Zorab said. "A fool and a fool. One to work, the other to clean house and cook."

19   "Perhaps," my grandfather said. "Can you cook, boy?"

20   "Of course he can cook," my grandmother said. "Rice, at least."

21   "Let the boy speak for himself," my grandfather said. "Is that true, boy, about the rice? Four cups of water, one cup of rice, a little spoon of salt. Do you know how to make it taste like food, and not swill, or am I dreaming?"

22   "I have cooked rice," Vask said. "It tasted like food. But it was salty. We had to drink water all day and all night."

23   "All right. It was salty," my grandfather said. "Of course you had to drink water all day and all night. We've all eaten rice like that." He turned to the others. He began to make faces again. "I think this is the boy to go," he said.

24   "On second thought," my uncle Zorab said, "two fools, one after the other, perhaps not. We have Aram here. I think he should go. Without question, he needs to be punished."

25   Everyone looked at me.

26   "Aram?" my grandfather said. "You mean the boy who laughs? You mean loud-laughing Aram Garoghlanian? What has the boy done to be punished like this?"

27   "*He knows*," my uncle Zorab said.

28   My grandfather looked at me. "What have you done, boy?"

29   I knew he was not angry with me. I began to laugh, remembering the things I had done. My grandfather listened for a minute, then began laughing with me. We were the only Garoghlanians in the world who laughed that way.

30   "Aram Garoghlanian," he said. "I say again: What have you done?"

31   "Which one?" I said.

32   "You know which one," my uncle Zorab said.

33   "Do you mean," I said, "telling all our friends that you are out of your mind?"

34   My uncle Zorab said nothing.

35   "Or do you mean," I said, "going around talking the way you talk?"

36   "This is the boy to send with Jorgi," uncle Zorab said.

37   "Can you cook rice?" my grandfather said.

38   I understood perfectly now. If I could cook rice, I could go with Jorgi to Hanford. I forgot about the writer who said a journey was a great thing. Fool or old or anything else, I *wanted* to go.

39   "I can cook rice," I said.

40   "Salty or swill, or what?" my grandfather said.

41   "Sometimes salty," I said. "Sometimes swill. Sometimes perfect."

42   "Let us think about this," my grandfather said. "Sometimes salty. Sometimes swill. Sometimes perfect. Is this the boy to send to Hanford?"

43   "Yes," my uncle Zorab said. "The only one."

44   "Then it is done," my grandfather said. "That will be all. I wish to be alone."

45   I started to go. My grandfather took me by the neck. "Stay a minute," he said. When we were alone, he said, "Talk the way your uncle Zorab talks."

46   I did, and my grandfather roared with laughter. "Go to Hanford," he said. "Go with the fool Jorgi and make it salty or make it swill or make it perfect."

II

47   We left the following morning before the sun was up. Sometimes Jorgi rode the bicycle and I walked, and sometimes I rode and Jorgi walked. We got to Hanford in the late afternoon.

48   The idea was for us to stay until Jorgi's job ended. So we looked around town for a house to live in. We found one that Jorgi liked and moved in that night. The house had eleven rooms, running water, and a kitchen. One room had two beds in it, and all the other rooms were empty. After we moved in, Jorgi took out his zither, sat on the floor, and began to play and sing. It was beautiful. It was sad sometimes and sometimes funny, but it was always beautiful. I don't know how long he played, but suddenly he got up off the floor and said, "Aram, I want rice."

49   I made rice that night that was both salty and swill, but my uncle Jorgi said, "Aram, this is wonderful."

50   The birds got us up with the sun.

51   "The job," I said. "You begin today, you know."

52   "Today," my uncle Jorgi said in a low, sad voice.

53   He walked slowly out of the empty house. I looked around for something to clean with, but found nothing. So I went out and sat on the steps to the front door. It seemed to be a nice part of the world in daylight. It was a street with only four houses. There was a church across the street from one of the houses. I sat on the steps for about an hour. My uncle Jorgi came up the street on his bicycle. The bicycle was going all over the place, and my uncle Jorgi was laughing and singing.

54   "Not this year, thank God," he said. He fell off the bicycle into a large plant covered with flowers.

55   "What?" I said.

56   "There is no job," he said. "No job, thank God."

57   He smelled a flower.

58   "No job?" I said.

59   "No job, praise our Father above us."

60   "Why not?" I said.

61   "The watermelons," he said.

62   "What about them?" I said.

63   "The season is over," he said.

64   "That isn't true," I said.

65   "The season is over," my uncle Jorgi said. "Believe me, it is finished. Praise God, the watermelons are all gone. They have all been taken up."

66   "Who said so?" I said.

67   "The farmer himself. The farmer himself said so," my uncle Jorgi said.

68   "He just said that," I said. "He didn't want to hurt you. He just said that because he knew your heart wouldn't be in your work."

69   "Praise God," my uncle Jorgi said, "the whole season is over. All the big, beautiful watermelons have been taken up and put in the barn."

70   "Your father will break your head," I said. "What will we do? The season is just beginning."

71   "It's ended," my uncle Jorgi said. "We will live in this house a month and then go home. We have paid six dollars

for the house and we have money enough for rice. We will dream here a month and then go home."

72 My uncle Jorgi danced into the house to his zither. Before I could decide what to do about him, he was playing and singing. It was beautiful. I didn't try to make him leave the house and go back to the farm. I just sat on the steps and listened.

73 We stayed in the house a month and then went home. My grandmother was the first to see us.

74 "You two came home just in time," she said. "He's been roaring like a tiger. Give me the money."

75 "There is no money," I said.

76 "Did he work?" my grandmother said.

77 "No," I said. "He played and sang the whole time."

78 "How was your rice?" she said.

79 "Sometimes salty," I said. "Sometimes swill. Sometimes perfect. But he didn't work."

80 "His father mustn't know," she said. "I have money."

81 She got some money out of a pocket and put it in my hands.

82 "When he comes home," she said, "give him this money."

83 "I will do as you say," I said.

84 When my grandfather came home he began to roar.

85 "Home already?" he said. "Is the season ended so soon? Where is the money he got?"

86 I gave him the money.

87 "I won't have him singing all day," my grandfather roared. "Some things simply have to stop, in the end. You will read in a book that a father loves a foolish son more than his wise sons. Believe me, that writer is not married, and also he has no sons."

88 In the yard, under the flowering tree, my uncle Jorgi began to play and sing. My grandfather came to a dead stop and began to listen. He sat down in his big chair, and began to make faces.

89 I went into the kitchen to get three or four glasses of water because of last night's rice. When I came back to the living room, the old man was sitting back in his chair, asleep and smiling. His son Jorgi was singing praises to the whole world at the top of his sad, beautiful voice.

AFTER YOU READ THE STORY

A. Understanding the Main Ideas

If the sentence is true, write T next to it. If it is not true, write F for false. Then rewrite the sentence to make it true.

_____ 1. Jorgi went to Hanford because he wanted to work in the fields there.

_____ 2. The grandfather believed that money was more important than music.

_____ 3. Uncle Zorab thought he could punish Aram by sending him to Hanford with Jorgi.

_____ 4. Aram thought that only a fool would go to Hanford.

_____ 5. When Jorgi arrived in Hanford, the watermelon season was already over.

_____ 6. Jorgi spent the whole month in Hanford playing his zither and singing.

_____ 7. Aram's grandmother gave Aram some money for the work he did cleaning and cooking for Jorgi.

_____ 8. Aram's grandfather didn't like Jorgi's music.

_____ 9. Aram's rice was always salty.

B. Close Reading

Aram's grandfather often talks about what we can read in books. He believes that what we read in books isn't always true in real life. In this exercise, reread the grandfather's words about books, and then answer questions about them.

1. *"You will read in a book that a man can sit all day under a tree and play music on a zither and sing. Believe me, that writer is a fool."* (paragraph 3)
   Why does the grandfather think the writer is a fool? What does the grandfather think about men who play music, not in books, but in real life?

2. *"You will read in a book that a woman is a perfect and beautiful thing. Believe me, that writer is not looking at his wife."* (paragraph 7)

   What is the writer looking at? What did the grandmother say, in real life, to anger the grandfather?

3. *"You will read in a book that a journey to a new city is a great thing for a young man. That writer is probably a fool of eighty or ninety."* (paragraph 12)

   According to the grandfather, how many journeys did that writer probably make? What does the grandfather think about journeys to new places, not in books, but in real life?

4. *"You will read in a book that a father loves a foolish son more than his wise sons. Believe me, that writer is not married, and also he has no sons."* (paragraph 87)

   Does the grandfather love his foolish son, Jorgi? What does the grandfather do, in real life, when Jorgi begins to play his music?

C. Discussion

1. The paragraph about Saroyan on page 39 tells us that his family was a large and loving one. Do you think the family in "The Journey to Hanford" is a loving one? Why or why not?
2. The grandfather in the story is like the king of the family. His word is law. And he is the king mostly because he is the oldest man. Perhaps that was the way with families in his old country (Armenia). Do you know a family where the oldest man is like the king of the family? Do you think every family needs a king (or queen)? Why or why not?
3. Did this story make you laugh or smile in places? Which places?
4. What kind of work do you like best? What do you like to do when you are not working? What do you think about Jorgi's music: Is it play or work?

D. Vocabulary Practice

For each space in the following sentences, choose the best word from this list.

fool	season	praise	salty
punish	roar	journey	watermelon
zither	swill	perfect	

In this story, nothing is what it seems. For example, uncle Zorab thinks he will _____ Aram by sending him to Hanford with Jorgi. But Aram really likes the idea of a _____ to a new place. The grandfather says he doesn't want to hear Jorgi play any more music on his _____. But he begins to _____ like a tiger when the music stops. Jorgi goes to Hanford for a job in the _____ fields. But when he arrives, the farmer tells him that the _____ is over. Most important, although the grandfather tells everyone that Jorgi is a _____, his smile at the end of the story is the highest kind of _____ for his son. The only sure thing in this story is that Aram's rice will be sometimes _____, sometimes _____, and sometimes _____!

E. Word Forms

Study the chart below. Note the words that make nouns by adding *-tion, -ment,* or *-ness* to the verb form. Note the words that have no change between noun and verb form. Use the chart to help you choose the correct form of the word in parentheses to put in the blank space in the sentences below.

Noun	Verb	Adjective	Adverb
punishment	punish	punishing	punishingly
praise	praise		
perfection	perfect	perfect	perfectly
season		seasonal	
salt	salt	salty	
		salted	
fool, foolishness	fool	foolish	foolishly

1. (*punish*) For Aram, going on a journey with Jorgi was not a _____, but a joy.

2. (*praise*) Aram's rice that first night in Hanford was both salty and swill, but Jorgi _____ it.

3. (*perfect*) "Aram," he said, "this rice of yours was cooked to _____ !" Then he went to the kitchen and drank three glasses of water, one right after the other.

4. (*season*) "Watermelons are a _____ fruit," the farmer said to Jorgi. "And I'm sorry to say that now the _____ is over. It's finished. There is no job here for you."

5. (*salt*) On their last night in Hanford, Aram said, "Uncle Jorgi, I didn't _____ the rice enough. Let's add more!"

6. (*fool*) Who do you think was more _____: Zorab, Jorgi, the grandfather, or Aram? Or perhaps the farmer?

F. Language Activity: Interview About Immigrants

The paragraph about Saroyan on page 39 tells us that his family came to the United States from Armenia. They were *immigrants*, that is, people who moved from one country to another to live. The United States is sometimes called a country of immigrants because it is made up of people from all over the world. But all countries have immigrants. And the number of immigrants in many countries has grown in the past fifteen to twenty years.

For this exercise, talk to a person (inside or outside your class) who is not from this country. Find out about immigrants in that person's country. Some of the questions you could ask are these:

Are there many immigrants in your country?
Where do they come from?
Why do they come to your country?
How many of them are happy with their new country: not many of them? some of them? most of them? all of them?
What is the greatest difficulty they face in their new country: finding a place to live? finding a job? making friends? the change of weather or food? the love they have for their old country? something else?

To the questions above, add at least three of your own. Write down the questions you will ask. Write down at least parts of the answers you get. Report back to the class.

G. Writing: A Summary

To make a summary, we first read a piece of writing that has many words. Then we write in a few words the most important things that the many words said. Below is an example of a summary. It is a summary of Part I of "The Journey to Hanford."

Example:

Aram's family wanted Jorgi to go away for a while. The grandfather of the family thought Jorgi was foolish to play music and not get money. He sent Jorgi to Hanford to work in the watermelon fields. The family had a big meeting to decide which boy would go with Jorgi to cook and clean for him. The family almost decided that Aram's cousin Vask would go. But then Aram's uncle Zorab chose Aram. He thought he could punish Aram by sending him. But Aram wanted to go. He said he could cook rice for his uncle Jorgi, sometimes salty, sometimes swill, and sometimes perfect. The grandfather chose Aram.

Now, write a paragraph that is a summary of Part II of "The Journey to Hanford." Put in your summary the parts of the story you think are the most important. Your summary should include at least the following parts of the story:

- how they went to Hanford
- the kind of house they found to live in
- their first night there
- what Jorgi said when he came back from the farmer the next day
- how they spent the month in Hanford
- the grandmother and the money when they get home again
- the grandfather roaring
- then Jorgi playing his music

Add your own ideas of what is important in Part II. Try to write 80 to 120 words.

THE TELL-TALE HEART

Adapted from the story by
EDGAR ALLAN POE

Edgar Allan Poe was born in 1809 in Boston, Massachusetts. Poe's parents died when he was a little child. After that, he lived with a family named Allan. They moved to England for five years when Poe was six. Although he was an excellent student and swimmer as a boy and young man, Poe led a very unhappy, troubled life. He often fought with Mr. Allan, and finally separated from him at the age of twenty-two. Allan had become very rich, but Poe was poor for the rest of his life. He worked for magazines, but drank too much and lost many jobs. He married his young cousin, Virginia, but she became sick and died. Through all his difficulties, Poe never stopped writing, and his writing took many forms. He often wrote about the dark side of the human heart. He was interested in what lies between the real and the unreal in our lives. People remember Poe now for his poetry and for his dark, strange stories like "The Tell-Tale Heart." Poe died at the age of forty in 1849.

BEFORE YOU READ THE STORY

A. About the Author

1. Read the paragraph about Edgar Allan Poe on page 55. Do you think Poe had reasons to be unhappy? What were some of them?
2. A *tale* is a story. What do you think the title "The Tell-Tale Heart" means?

B. The Pictures

1. Look at the picture on page 58. What word can you use to describe the man's face? There is a light shining on the man's face. Where is the light coming from? What is the other person holding?
2. Three policemen are in the picture on page 62. What words can you use to describe their faces? Who are they looking at?

C. Thinking About It

What do you think small children are most afraid of? the dark? large, strange animals? sudden, loud noises? things they do not understand? What were you afraid of when you were very young? Are older people afraid of the same things? Do most people talk easily about their fears? Why or why not?

D. Skimming

Take sixty seconds to skim "The Tell-Tale Heart." (Quickly read the first two or three sentences of each paragraph.) Do not look at the story again. Now look at the three groups of words below. Which group fits the general idea you got from skimming the story—A, B, or C?

A	B	C
machine	flower	house
tomorrow	today	yesterday
study	enjoy	kill
new	young	old
thinking	happy	mad
noon	morning	midnight

careful Be *careful* crossing the street! And please use that knife *carefully*. I don't want you to cut yourself.

horrible The bloody, dead cat was *horrible* to see. The dog showed its teeth, then opened its mouth and made a *horrible* sound.

mad This word has many meanings. It is often used to mean "angry," but in "The Tell-Tale Heart," *mad* means "out of his mind" or "crazy." A *madman* is a man who has lost his mind, so he does very strange things.

nervous He felt *nervous* before the big game, on the first day at his job, and when they opened his bags at Customs. Alone on a dark street at night, he looked around *nervously*.

THE TELL-TALE HEART

True! Nervous. I was nervous then and I am nervous now. But why do you say that I am mad? Nothing was wrong with me. I could see very well. I could smell. I could touch. Yes, my friend, and I could hear. I could hear all things in the skies and in the earth. So why do you think that I am mad? Listen. I will tell you the story. I will speak quietly. You will understand everything. Listen!

2   Why did I want to kill the old man? Ah, this is very difficult. I liked the old man. No, I loved him! He never hurt me. He was always kind to me. I didn't need his gold; no, I didn't want that. I think it was his eye—yes, it was this! He had the eye of a bird. It was a cold, light-blue eye—a horrible eye. I feared it. Sometimes I tried to look at it. But then my blood ran cold. So, after many weeks, I knew I must kill the old man. His horrible eye must not live. Do you understand?

3   Now here is the point. You think that I am mad. Madmen know nothing. But I? I was careful. Oh, I was very

careful. *Careful*, you see? For one long week, I was very kind to the old man. But every night, at midnight, I opened his door slowly, carefully. I had a lantern with me. Inside the lantern there was a light. But the sides of the lantern hid the light. So, first I put the dark lantern through the open door. Then I put my head in the room. I put it in slowly, very slowly. I didn't want to wake the old man. Ha! Would a madman be careful, like that? There was no noise, not a sound. I opened the lantern carefully—very carefully—and slowly. A thin light fell upon the old man's eye. I held it there. I held it there for a long time. And I did this every night for seven nights. But always the eye was closed. And so I could not do my work. I was not angry at the old man, you see. I was angry only at his horrible eye. And every morning I went into his room happily. I was friendly with him. I asked about his night. Did he sleep well? Was he all right? And so, you see, he knew nothing.

4   On the eighth night, I was more careful than before. I know you don't believe me, but it is true. The clock's hand moved more quickly than my hand. I opened the door slowly. I put the lantern in the room. The old man moved suddenly in his bed. But I did not go back. The room was very dark. I knew he could not see me. I put my head in the room. I began to open the lantern, but my hand hit the side. It made a loud noise.

5   The old man sat up quickly in bed. "Who's there?" he cried.

6   I stood still and said nothing. For one long hour I did not move a finger. And he did not lie down. He sat in his bed. He listened. I knew his fear!

7   And soon I heard another sound. It came from the old man. It was a horrible sound, the sound of fear! I knew that sound well. Often, at night, I too have made that sound. What was in the room? The old man didn't know. He didn't want to know. But he knew that he was in danger. Ah, yes, he knew!

8   And now I began to open the lantern. I opened it just a little. A small thin light fell upon the horrible blue eye.

9   It was open—wide, wide open. I could not see the old man's face or body. But I saw the eye very well. The horrible bird's eye. My blood ran cold. At the same time, anger began to grow inside me.

10   And now, haven't I told you that I could hear everything? Now a low, quick sound came to my ears. It was like the sound of a small wooden clock. I knew *that* sound well, too. It was the beating of the old man's heart!

11   My fear and anger grew. But I did not move. I stood still. I held the light on the old man's eye. And the beating of the heart grew. It became quicker and quicker, and louder and louder every second! I knew that his fear was very great. *Louder*, do you hear? I have told you that I am nervous. And this is true. My fear was like the old man's. But I did not move. I held the light on his eye. But the beating grew louder, LOUDER! And now a new fear came to me. Someone in the next house would hear! The old man must die! This was his hour! With a loud cry, I opened the lantern wide. I ran into the room! The old man cried loudly once—once only. His fear, his fear killed him! In a second I pulled him from the bed. He lay still. I smiled a little. Everything was all right. For some minutes, I heard his heart beat softly. Then it stopped. I put my hand on his body. He was cold. He was like a stone. The old man was dead. His eye would never look upon me again!

12   And now I was very, very careful. I worked quickly but quietly. I used a good, new knife. I cut off the old man's arms and legs and head. Then I took three boards from the floor of the room. I put everything below the floor. Then I put the boards in their place again. I cleaned the floor. There was no blood. Nothing was wrong. I was *careful*, you see? Ha! Can you still think that I am mad?

13   I finished. It was four o'clock—still dark as midnight. Suddenly there was a beating on the door. Someone was there. But I went down with a happy heart. I had nothing to fear. Nothing.

14   Three policemen came into the house. They said that someone in the next house heard a cry. Was something wrong? Was everyone all right?

15   "Of course," I said. "Please come in." I was not nervous. I smiled at the men. I told them that the old man was in another town. I said he was with his sister. I showed them his money, his gold. Everything was there, in its place.

16   I brought chairs. I asked the men to sit. I sat, too. I sat on the boards over the dead man's body! I talked easily. The policemen smiled.

17   But after some minutes I became tired. Perhaps I was a little nervous. There was a low sound in my head, in my ears. I didn't like it. I talked more loudly, more angrily. Then suddenly I understood. The sound was not in my head or in my ears. It was there in the room!

18   Now I know that I became *very* nervous. *It was a low, quick sound. It sounded like a small wooden clock*! My eyes opened wide. Could the policemen hear it? I talked in a louder voice. But the noise did not stop. It grew! I stood up and talked angrily, dangerously. I walked across the floor and back again. Why wouldn't the men leave? There was a storm inside my head! And still the noise became louder— LOUDER—LOUDER! I beat my hands on the table. I said dangerous things in a loud voice. But still the men talked happily and smiled. Couldn't they hear? Was it possible? Oh, God! No, no! They heard! They knew! They laughed at my hopes, and smiled at my fears. I knew it then and I know it now. I couldn't keep still! Anything was better than their smiles and laughing! And now—again!—listen! louder! LOUDER! LOUDER!

19   "Stop!" I cried. "Enough! Enough! Pull up the boards! Below the floor! Here, here!—It is the beating of his horrible heart!"

AFTER YOU READ THE STORY

A. Understanding the Main Ideas

Complete each sentence below by choosing **a**, **b**, or **c**. The first half of each sentence tells about something that happened in the story (*the effect*). The second half tells why it happened (*the cause*).

1. The young man wanted to kill the old man because
   a. he loved the old man.
   b. he didn't like the old man's eye.
   c. he wanted the old man's gold.

2. He opened the old man's door carefully because
   a. the old man was mad.
   b. he thought the old man was horrible.
   c. he didn't want to wake the old man.

3. Every morning the young man was friendly because
   a. he held a thin light over the old man's eye.
   b. he didn't want the old man to think anything was wrong.
   c. he was angry at the old man.

4. The police came to the house because
   a. someone in the next house heard a cry.
   b. they knew the young man was mad.
   c. they wanted to sit, talk, and laugh.

5. The young man talked louder and louder to the police because
   a. he thought they couldn't hear him.
   b. he thought they would hear the beating of the old man's heart.
   c. he thought they would understand him and leave.

6. The young man killed the old man and then told the police because
   a. the old man laughed and smiled at him.
   b. the police heard the beating of the old man's heart.
   c. the young man was mad.

B. Close Reading

The first half of a sentence is in column A. Match it with the phrase in column B that completes the meaning of the sentence. The first one is done for you.

A	B
_c_ 1. The madman thought	a. when he heard a low, quick sound.
____ 2. He wanted to kill the old man	b. after the young man ran into the room.
____ 3. The old man woke up	c. that he could hear all things in the skies and in the earth.
____ 4. The old man died	d. when the young man's hand hit the lantern.
____ 5. The young man told the police	e. because he was afraid of the beating of the heart below the floor.

_____ 6. The young man
became nervous

f. that the old man was in
another town.

_____ 7. He told the police
about the killing

g. because he hated his cold,
blue eye.

C. Discussion

1. The old man was dead. His body, in pieces, was below the floor. But the young man believed that he could hear the old man's heart beating. Why?
2. What do you think will happen to the man after the police take him away? Should he go to prison? to a doctor? Should he be killed?
3. Were you afraid while you read "The Tell-Tale Heart"? This kind of story is called a _horror_ story. Do you enjoy horror stories? Do you enjoy horror movies? Why, or why not?

D. Vocabulary Practice

Complete the sentences in a way that shows the meaning of the underlined word. The paragraphs where the word appears are in parentheses. This exercise asks you to tell what you think about Poe's story.

1. I was sure the young man was <u>mad</u> when he _____

_____.

(paragraphs 1 and 3)

2. The thing that was most <u>horrible</u> for me in the story was ___

_____.

(paragraphs 2, 3, and 19)

3. I felt some <u>fear</u> when _____

_____.

(paragraphs 2, 6, and 11)

4. When he was with the police, the most <u>dangerous</u> thing the young man did was _____

_____ .

(paragraph 18)

5. I think the young man was <u>nervous</u> at the beginning of the story because _____

_____ .

(paragraphs 1 and 11)

E. Word Forms

Sometimes the noun form of a word seems very different from the adjective and adverb forms. Look at the chart below.

Noun	Adjective	Adverb
horror	horrible	horribly
nerve	nervous	nervously
care	careful	carefully
danger	dangerous	dangerously

Choose the correct form of the word in parentheses to complete each sentence correctly.

1. (*horrible / horror*) The old man's eye seemed _____ to the young man. It filled him with _____ .

2. (*care / carefully*) He didn't want to make any noise, so he opened the lantern _____ . He took _____ not to make the smallest sound.

3. (*danger / dangerous*) The young man knew he was in _____ from the police. And the police thought the young man might be _____ , so they were careful in the way they spoke to him.

4. (*nerves / nervously*) The young man spoke more and more _____ because his _____ were highly excited.

F. Language Activity: Using Similes

Look at these sentences from the story:

"He was cold. He was like a stone." (paragraph 11)
"It sounded like a small wooden clock." (paragraph 18)

In these sentences, the writer uses *similes*. That is, he helps us understand one thing or idea or action by showing us something similar—something *like* the thing or idea or action. We understand that *the cold* was a cold *like stone*—but not, for example, like ice. We understand that the *low, quick sound* was a sound *like a wooden clock*—that is, fast and with the same amount of time between each sound.

In the sentences below, choose the best way to complete each sentence. Be ready to tell why you think it is the best. Then, try to think of an even better ending.

1. When the young man opened the lantern, he was very careful. He moved like
   a. a dog.
   b. a cat.
   c. a bird.

2. When the police came into the house, they filled the young man with fear. They looked down on him with strong faces (see the picture on page 62). They seemed like
   a. unmoving mountains.
   b. strong rivers.
   c. tall trees in a wind.

3. For one long week, he was very kind to the old man. To the old man, he was like
   a. a white star.
   b. the cold moon.
   c. the warm sun.

4. The old man's horrible heart beat louder and LOUDER and LOUDER! The sound was like
   a. a cloudy sky.
   b. a stormy sea.
   c. a wet field.

5. The young man talked nervously to the police. His voice was strange. He sounded like
   a. an old radio.
   b. running water.
   c. a heavy car.

G. Writing: A Police Report

You are one of the policemen in "The Tell-Tale Heart." You must write a report about the killing. In your report, answer the following questions. An answer to the first question is given.

Example:

What time was it when you went to the old man's house?
It was 5:00 A.M. when I went to the old man's house.

Why did you go there?
Who met you at the door?
How did he seem—friendly? nervous? angry?
Did he ask you to come in?
Did you ask about the old man?
What did he say about the old man?
Where did he take you?
Did he ask you to sit, or to stand?
Did he sit, or stand?
How did he talk?
After some minutes of this, how did he seem?
How did he talk then?
Finally, what did he say?
What did you find below the boards?
What happened then?

6

TOM WHITEWASHES THE FENCE

Adapted from the story by

MARK TWAIN

Mark Twain's real name was Samuel Langhorne Clemens. He was born in 1835 in a small town in Missouri, on the Mississippi River. When he was twelve, his father died, and he went to work for a printer. He began writing humorous stories when he was seventeen. He became a pilot (or driver) of steamboats on the Mississippi River in 1858. When the War between the States stopped boats from traveling on the river, Clemens became a soldier in the southern army. But he soon left the army, and in 1861 he went out West to look for gold and adventure. There, he became a newspaper reporter. In 1863 he began writing under the name of Mark Twain. ("Mark Twain" was a phrase used on riverboats to mean "12 feet (4 yards) deep.") In 1866, Twain moved to Connecticut, where he wrote the books that made him famous. He is best known today for his two novels about boys growing up in small towns along the Mississippi: *The Adventures of Tom Sawyer* and *The Adventures of Huckleberry Finn*. Twain traveled widely in the United States and Europe. In the last years of his life, he became famous as a public speaker. He died in 1910.

A. About the Author

Read the paragraph about Mark Twain on page 69. What different kinds of work did he do during his long life (how many different jobs can you find in the paragraph)? From which of his jobs did he take the name "Mark Twain"?

B. The Pictures

Look at the picture on page 73. How much of the fence has new paint? What is on the river in the distance? Now look at the picture on page 76. How much of the fence is painted now? Tom is looking at a group of things. What are they? Are they Tom's? How do you think he got them?

C. Thinking About It

"Tom Whitewashes the Fence" is from Twain's novel *The Adventures of Tom Sawyer*. Early in the novel, we learn that Tom's mother and father are dead. Tom lives with Aunt Polly, her son Sid, and Jim, a young man who works for the family. Tom is always getting into trouble, and sometimes Aunt Polly punishes him. Did you ever get into trouble when you were younger? What did you do? How were you punished?

D. Scanning for Numbers

Scan the paragraph about Twain on page 69 to find the numbers that answer the following questions.

1. How old was Twain when his father died?
2. What did he begin doing at the age of seventeen?
3. When did Twain became a steamboat pilot?
4. In what year did he take the name "Mark Twain" as a writer?
5. In what year did Twain leave the West?
6. How old was Twain when he died?

fence, boards, whitewash, bucket, brush   All these words are used in the story to describe a job that the boy, Tom, must do. Tom's house has a *fence* around it. The *fence* is made of wooden *boards*. The *boards* are painted white, and sometimes need to be repainted. The white paint Tom uses is called *whitewash*. Tom carries the *whitewash* in a *bucket* and paints the *fence* with a large *brush*.

marbles, kite   A *marble* is a small round ball made of glass or stone, used in an old children's game. A *kite* is made of paper and sticks of wood, and you fly it in the wind at the end of a string. *Marbles* and *kites* are playthings.

TOM WHITEWASHES
THE FENCE

Tom got home very late one night. When he climbed carefully in at the window, he found his Aunt Polly waiting for him. She had fire in her eyes. And when she saw his dirty clothes, she decided then and there to punish him. Tomorrow was a free Saturday, but Tom would have to spend it hard at work, she told him.

2   Tomorrow came. And that Saturday morning was beautiful in the village. All the summer world was bright and fresh and full of life. There was a song in every heart. And if the heart was young, the song was sung out loud. The trees were covered with flowers and the air smelled sweet. Beyond the village the hills were green, just far enough away to seem dreamy, restful, and inviting.

3   Tom appeared on the road with a bucket of whitewash and a long brush. He looked at the fence. All gladness left him, and a deep sadness fell on his heart. Thirty yards of board fence, nine feet high. Suddenly Tom's life seemed hard and empty. Sadly he dipped his brush in the whitewash. He painted part of a board at the top of the fence. He did it

again. And again. Only a few feet of white board on a whole world of unwhitewashed fence. He sat down on the road-side, discouraged.

4   Jim came out of the house, singing "Buffalo Gals." He was carrying the water bucket. Tom had always thought that bringing water from the town well was hateful work. But now it didn't seem so bad. He remembered there was always a crowd at the well. Boys and girls—white, black, and brown—played and fought, rested and traded play-things while they waited to get water. The well was only a hundred and fifty yards away. But Jim never got back with a bucket of water in less than an hour. And even then, some-body usually had to go get him.

5   Maybe if he offered Jim something special, Jim would trade places with him.

6   "Say, Jim," said Tom. "I'll get the water if you white-wash some."

7   Jim shook his head and said, "I can't, Tom. Your Aunt Polly, she says I've got to get this water. She says she expects Tom will try to ask me to whitewash."

8   "Oh, never mind what Aunt Polly says, Jim. That's the way she always talks. Give me the bucket. I won't be gone more than a minute. She won't ever know. I'll trade you my white marble, Jim."

9   "Wel-l-l . . ."

10   This invitation was too much for him. He put down the water bucket and reached for Tom's white marble. Suddenly they heard the sound of a door opening and shutting. Aunt Polly had come out of the house. In another moment, Jim was running down the road with his bucket, and Tom was painting with energy. Aunt Polly went back into the house with triumph in her eye.

11   But Tom's energy did not continue for very long. He began to think of the fun he had planned for this Saturday. Soon the free boys would come running along on their deli-cious adventures. They would make fun of him for having to work. The thought of this burnt Tom like fire. He got out all his treasures and looked at them. He had only some bits of toys and a few marbles. It was enough to trade for *work*, maybe, but not enough to buy even half an hour of freedom. He gave up the idea of trying to buy the boys. Then, at this

dark and hopeless moment, an idea broke upon him. A grand, triumphant idea!

12   Tom dipped in his brush and peacefully went to work. Soon Ben Rogers came down the road. Ben Rogers—the one boy, of all boys, who would most enjoy making fun of Tom. Ben was running and jumping; his heart was light, and he was eating an apple. From time to time, he gave out a musical cry, followed by a deeper "ding-dong-dong, ding-dong-dong." He was pretending to be a steamboat. As he came near, he slowed his speed and took the middle of the street. He bent far to his right and then began to turn in a very slow but grand circle. He was pretending to be not just any steamboat, but the *Big Missouri*. The *Big Missouri* was a large, beautiful, and famous steamboat with two big water wheels. Ben was boat and captain and engine bells all at once. He turned and came slowly toward Tom.

13   "Stop her, sir! Ting-a-ling!" Ben came nearer the fence. He was bringing the big boat to land.

14   "Get ready to back the engines! Ting-a-ling!" He held his arms straight down by his sides. "Back now on the right wheel! Chow! ch-chow-wow! Chow!" He pretended his right arm was a forty-foot water wheel, and began to move it in a slow circle.

15   "Back now on the left wheel! Ting-a-ling! Chow ch-chow-chow! Chow!" Now the left hand started the wide circle.

16   "Stop the right! Ting-a-ling! Stop the left! Come ahead on the right! Stop her! Let her turn slow! Ting-a-ling! Chow-ow-ow! Get ready to throw the lines! *Quickly* now! You down there, what are you doing?! Tie the lines over there! Stand by to shut down! Done with the engines, sir! Ting-a-ling! Sh! Sh! Shhhhhh!" The steamboat came to a stop.

17   Tom went on whitewashing. He was paying no attention to the steamboat. Ben watched Tom a moment. Then he said, "Hello, old boy. *You're* in trouble, hey?"

18   No answer. Tom stepped back and looked at his work with the eye of an artist. He dipped in his brush and painted a few feet of board. He stepped back and looked carefully, as before. Ben came up beside him. Tom's mouth watered for Ben's apple, but he kept on working.

19   Ben said: "Hi there, Tom. You got to work, hey?"

20   Tom turned slowly and said, "Why, it's you, Ben. I didn't notice."

21   "Say, *I'm* going swimming, I am. Don't you wish you could? But, of course, you'd rather *work*, wouldn't you? Of *course* you would."

22   Tom looked at Ben peacefully. "What do you call work?"

23   "Well, isn't *that* work?"

24   Tom continued whitewashing. He answered happily, "Well, maybe it is, and maybe it isn't. All I know is that it's good for Tom Sawyer."

25   "Oh, come on, now," said Ben. "You don't mean you *like* it?"

26   Tom's brush continued to paint. "Like it?" he answered. "Well, I don't see why I shouldn't like it. Does a boy get a chance to whitewash a fence every day?"

27   That showed the work in a new light. Ben stopped eating his apple. Tom lightly touched the wood with his brush. He stepped back to look at the new effect—added another touch here and there—studied the effect again. Ben was watching every move. He was getting more and more interested.

28   After a few moments he said, "Say, Tom, let *me* whitewash a little."

29   Tom pretended to think about Ben's offer. He seemed to agree. But then he said, "No—no, I don't think that will work, Ben. You see, Aunt Polly cares a lot about this fence. It's right in front, you know. If it was the back fence, I wouldn't mind, and *she* wouldn't. Yes, this job has to be done very carefully. Why, I don't think a boy in a thousand—maybe two thousand—can do it the way it ought to be done."

30   "No—is that right? Oh come on, Tom, let me just try. Only just a little. I'd let *you* try if it was me, Tom."

31   "Ben, I'd like to, really I would, but Aunt Pollly . . . Jim wanted to paint, and my cousin Sid, and she wouldn't let them. You see my problem? If you started painting and something happened to the fence . . ."

32   "Oh, Tom, I'd be real careful. Let me try. Say, Tom," he said invitingly, "I'll give you a bite of my apple."

33   "Well, here—No, Ben, now don't. I'm afraid . . ."

34   "I'll give you *all* of it!"

35   Tom gave up the brush with worry in his face but triumph in his heart. And while the big steamboat worked hard in the sun, the famous artist sat on the grass in the shade. He ate Ben's apple and waited for the next boy. Plenty of boys came down the road as the day passed. They came to make fun of him, but they stayed to whitewash. When Ben got tired, Tom traded the next chance to Billy Fisher. Billy gave Tom his kite to fly. And when Billy got tired, Johnny Miller bought some time with a dead rat tied on a string to pull it by. By the end of the afternoon Tom was no longer the poor boy he had been that morning. In fact, he was swimming in treasures. Besides the kite and the rat, he had twelve marbles, a piece of blue glass to look through, a key that wouldn't unlock anything, a toy soldier, four pieces of orange peel, two small fish in a can, part of a knife, a little black cat, a box of wooden matches, and the bottom half of an old window.

36   He had a nice, good restful time all the while. There were plenty of boys there to talk with and play with. And the fence had three coats of whitewash on it. If he'd had more whitewash he could have gotten all the treasures in the village.

37   Tom said to himself that it was not such an empty world, after all. He had discovered a great law of human action, without knowing it. That is, to make a man or a boy want something, it is only necessary to make it difficult to get. If Tom had been great and wise, like the writer of this story, he would understand that work is whatever somebody *has* to do, and play is whatever somebody *doesn't* have to do.

38   Tom thought about how and why his luck had changed. Then he went inside to report to Aunt Polly.

AFTER YOU READ THE STORY

A. Understanding the Main Ideas

Below are four key sentences from the story. Answer the question after each one.

1. *"All gladness left him, and a deep sadness fell on his heart."* (paragraph 3)
   Why did Tom feel so sad?

2. *"Then, at this dark and hopeless moment, an idea broke upon him. A grand, triumphant idea!"* (paragraph 11)

What was Tom's grand, triumphant idea?

3. *"By the end of the afternoon Tom was no longer the poor boy he had been that morning."* (paragraph 35)

What did he have at the end of the day that he didn't have at the beginning?

4. *"He had discovered a great law of human action. . . ."* (paragraph 37)

What was this "law"?

B. Close Reading

We use six question words to get most of the information we need to know about an action, event, or story. They are *what, when, where, why, how,* and *who.* Try to answer the questions below from memory. If you can't remember a particular piece of information, read the story more closely until you find it.

1. When does the story take place?
2. Why does Tom have to whitewash the fence?
3. Where is Jim going when he comes out of the house?
4. How does Tom paint the fence when Ben comes near?
5. What does Ben trade for the brush?
6. Who gives Tom a kite for the brush?

C. Discussion

1. In the story (paragraphs 12–16), Ben pretends to be a steamboat. He does this by moving in strange ways, and by making sounds. When you were young, did you pretend to be certain people, machines, or things? What were they? Do you still pretend to be other people or things? When and why?
2. Review the list of "treasures" that Tom has at the end of the story (paragraph 35). These were boys' treasures in an American village 150 years ago. What are boys' treasures in your town today? What about girls' treasures?
3. What do you think about the "law" that Tom discovers that day (paragraph 37)? Do you think this law is true in real life today? Give examples to show what you think. What do you think about Twain's words about work and play: ". . . work is whatever somebody *has* to do, and play is whatever somebody *doesn't* have to do." Is this true in your own life?

D. Vocabulary Practice

In the sentences below, underline one of the two words or phrases in each pair, to make a true sentence about the story. The first one is done for you.

Example:

Tom (*traded* / *painted*) the (*fence* / *bucket*).

1. The far-away hills were (*discouraging* / *inviting*), but Tom could not go there; he had no (*freedom* / *whitewash*) that Saturday. His place was near the (*fence* / *steamboat*).

2. Tom used his long (*brush* / *boards*) like (*an artist* / *a pilot*).

3. Tom (*pretended* / *traded*) to like whitewashing the fence, and finally Ben (*pretended to be* / *traded*) an apple for some time with the (*brush* / *kite*).

4. Tom was (*pretending* / *discouraged*) at the start of the day, but by the end of the day there was a look of (*worry* / *triumph*) on his face. He had discovered a great (*law* / *kite and marble*).

E. Word Forms

The adjective form of some words is made by adding *-ful* to the noun form; the adverb form of these words is made by adding *-fully* to the noun form. For example:

Noun	Adjective	Adverb
rest	restful	restfully
care	careful	carefully
law	lawful	lawfully
hate	hateful	hatefully
peace	peaceful	peacefully

The sentences below are from the story. Choose the correct form of the word to complete each one. Try to do the exercise without looking at the story. The paragraph number is given if you need help.

1. (*rest* / *restful* / *restfully*) "Beyond the village the hills were green, just far enough away to seem dreamy, _____, and inviting. (paragraph 2) He had a nice, good _____ time all the while." (paragraph 36)

2. (*hate / hateful / hatefully*) "Tom had always thought that bringing water from the town well was _____ work." (paragraph 4)

3. (*peace / peaceful / peacefully*) "Tom dipped in his brush and _____ went to work." (paragraph 12)

4. (*care / careful / carefully*) "Yes, this job has to be done very _____." (paragraph 29)

5. (*law / lawful / lawfully*) "He had discovered a great _____ of human action, without knowing it." (paragraph 37)

F. Language Activity: Colorful Language

Read these sentences from the story.

". . . he found his Aunt Polly waiting for him. She had **fire in her eyes**." (paragraph 1)

"All the summer world was bright and fresh and full of life. There was a **song in every heart**." (paragraph 2)

Sometimes we use a word or phrase not in its exact sense, but to show us something that is *like* it. In the sentences above, we understand that Aunt Polly is *angry* by the *fire in her eyes*. We understand that the people in the village are *happy* with the beautiful Saturday morning because of the *song in every heart*.

Each sentence below contains an example of this kind of color-ful language. From the choices that follow each sentence, choose the one that best explains the meaning of the underlined phrase.

1. "Soon the free boys would come running along <u>on their delicious adventures</u>." (paragraph 11)

   a. The boys wanted food.
   b. The boys thought the day would be full and good.
   c. The boys would have adventures with food.

2. "They would make fun of him for having to work. The thought of this <u>burnt Tom like fire</u>." (paragraph 11)

    a. The thought made his face red.
    b. The thought made him cry out with pain.
    c. The thought made him laugh.

3. "Then, at this dark and hopeless moment, <u>an idea broke upon him. A grand, triumphant idea</u>!" (paragraph 11)

    a. It was like a broken bone.
    b. It was like a pain in his heart.
    c. It was like a bright light in his mind.

4. "That showed the work <u>in a new light</u>." (paragraph 27)

    a. The work looked clearer to Ben.
    b. The work looked different, and better, to Ben.
    c. The work looked newer to Ben.

5. "Tom gave up the brush <u>with worry in his face but triumph in his heart</u>." (paragraph 35)

    a. He was happy, but he was worried, too.
    b. He was happy, but he pretended to worry.
    c. He was worried, but he looked happy.

6. "In fact, he <u>was swimming in treasures</u>." (paragraph 35)

    a. He had a lot of treasures.
    b. He took the treasures to the river to swim with them.
    c. The treasures were wet with rainwater.

G. Writing: A Dialog

At the end of the story, Twain tells us: "Tom thought about how and why his luck had changed. Then he went inside to report to Aunt Polly." In this exercise, you are asked to write Tom's half of his talk with Aunt Polly. Be sure to answer all of Aunt Polly's questions. Read your dialog out loud with another person to make sure it makes sense and seems natural.

Tom comes into the house carrying a box with all his new treasures.

Aunt Polly: (*calls*) Tom? Is that you? (*comes closer*) Have you finished the fence?

Tom: _____

Aunt Polly: Did you do a good job? How does the fence look?

Tom: _____

Aunt Polly: Oh, good. I'm glad you took the job seriously. Tell me now, what do you have in that box?

Tom: _____

Aunt Polly: Let me look. Goodness! Where did you get all those things, Tom? Did you find them, or take them, or did someone give them to you?

Tom: _____

Aunt Polly: What? Now tell me the truth, Tom. What did you do?

Tom: _____

Aunt Polly: I don't understand. Tell me—who painted the fence in the end?

Tom: _____

Aunt Polly: Well, I never! And now what? Will you give these things back to the boys?

Tom: _____

Aunt Polly: Tom, I asked you to paint the fence on your free day because I wanted you to learn something. And did you? What did you learn from painting the fence, Tom?

Tom: _____

_____

7

A WHITE HERON

Adapted from the story by
SARAH ORNE JEWETT

Sarah Orne Jewett was born in 1849 in South Berwick, Maine. She lived there quietly near the sea most of her life. Her father was a doctor. As a child, she went with him on his trips to see sick people in Maine's fishing and farm villages. She learned more this way than she learned at school, which she didn't like. She also learned by reading the many books in her parents' house. She began writing stories when she was very young. All her stories were about the simple lives of the country people she had met on her trips with her father. Her stories show her love of nature as well as human nature. The woods, fields, and animals of Maine are almost like characters in her stories. Her best-known book is called *Country of the Pointed Firs*. (Maine is well known for its pine and fir trees—evergreens, as they are called.) In 1909, Sarah Orne Jewett died in the same house in which she had been born and raised.

BEFORE YOU READ THE STORY

A. About the Author

Read the paragraph about Sarah Orne Jewett on page 83. What subjects does she write about? Where do her stories take place? Can you think of another writer in this book who wrote mostly about one particular place?

B. The Pictures

1. The bird in the picture on page 89 is a white heron. Why do you think the girl might have climbed a tree to see it? The tree in the picture is called a pine tree, a kind of tree that stays green all year.
2. The man in the picture on page 86 is a hunter, a man who follows wild animals in order to catch or kill them. Do you think the three people in this picture are a family? Why, or why not?

C. Thinking About It

"A White Heron" takes place more than 100 years ago. The story's main characters live deep in the country, far from cities or towns or even villages. How do you feel about the country? Have you spent time there? Would you like to live there? Which do you prefer, the city or the country? Why?

D. Skimming

Look over the following questions. Then skim the story. Read only the first sentence or two of each paragraph. Next, return to the questions below and write an answer to each one. Do not reread. Write only from memory. Complete the exercise in no more than five minutes. Compare your answers to those of another student.

1. Are the woman and the girl rich, or poor?
2. What does the girl, Sylvia, know a lot about?
3. What does the young man want?
4. Do you think Sylvia likes the young man?
5. Do you think you will enjoy reading the story? Why, or why not?

halloa   *Halloa* is an old-fashioned way of saying "hello."

nest   A *nest* is the home a bird builds from grass, small pieces of wood, and other materials.

step round   *Step round* is an old-fashioned way of saying "hurry up."

stuff (v.), stuffing (n.)   In this story, *stuffing* is the material put inside a dead animal to make it an object for scientific study. The hunter in the story *stuffs* birds so that people can study them outside of nature.

toad   A *toad* is a greenish-brown animal about the size of a large egg. It can live both on land and in the water. It has no tail, and its skin is very rough. It doesn't walk, it jumps. It eats insects. Many people think toads are ugly (the opposite of beautiful).

A WHITE HERON

I

The woods were already filled with shadows one June evening just before eight o'clock. Sylvia was driving her cow home. They turned deep into the dark woods. Their feet knew the way. The birds in the trees above her head seemed to sing "good night" to each other quietly. The air was soft and sweet. Sylvia felt a part of the gray shadows and the moving leaves. To Sylvia, it seemed as if she hadn't really been alive before she came to live with her grandmother in this beautiful place.

2   Suddenly she heard a call. Not a bird's call, which would have had a friendly sound. It was a young man's call, sudden and loud. Sylvia left the cow alone and hid behind some leaves. But the young man saw her.

3   "Halloa, little girl. How far is it to the road?"

4   Sylvia was afraid. She answered in a soft voice, "A good ways . . ."

5   "I'm hunting for some birds," the young man said kindly. He carried a gun over his shoulder. "I am lost and

need a friend very much. Don't be afraid. Speak up, and tell me what your name is. Do you think I can spend the night at your house and go out hunting in the morning?"

6   Sylvia was more afraid than ever. But she said her name, and dropped her head like a broken flower.

7   Her grandmother was waiting at the door. The cow gave a "moo" as the three arrived.

8   "Yes, you should speak for yourself, you old cow," said her grandmother. "Where was she hiding so long, Sylvy?"

9   Sylvia didn't speak. She thought her grandmother should be afraid of the stranger.

10   But the young man stood his gun beside the door. He dropped a heavy gun-bag beside it. He said good evening and told the old woman his story.

11   "Dear me, yes," she answered. "You might do better if you went out to the road a mile away. But you're welcome to what we've got. I'll milk the cow right away. Now, you make yourself at home. Sylvy, step round, and set a plate for the gentleman!"

12   Sylvia stepped. She was glad to have something to do, and she was hungry.

13   The young man was surprised to find such a comfortable, clean house in the deep woods of Maine. He thought this was the best supper he had eaten in a month. After supper the new-made friends sat in the shadowed doorway to watch the moon come up. The young man listened happily to the grandmother's stories. The old woman talked most about her children. About her daughter, Sylvia's mother, who had a hard life with so many children. About her son, Dan, who left home for California many years ago.

14   "Sylvy is like Dan," she said happily. "She knows every foot of the woods. She plays with the woods animals and feeds the birds. Yes, she'd give her own meals to them, if I didn't watch her!"

15   "So Sylvy knows all about birds, does she?" asked the young man. "I am trying to catch one of every kind."

16   "Do you keep them alive?" asked the old woman.

17   "No. I stuff them in order to save them," he answered. "I have almost a hundred of them. And I caught every one myself."

18   Sylvia was watching a toad jump in the moonlight.

19   "I followed a bird here that I want to catch. A white heron. You would know a heron if you saw it, Sylvy," he said, hopefully. "A strange, tall white bird with long, thin legs."

20   Sylvia's heart stopped. She knew that strange white bird.

21   "I want that bird more than anything," the young man went on. "I would give ten dollars to know where its nest is."

22   Sylvia couldn't believe there was so much money in the world. But she watched the toad and said nothing.

23   The next day Sylvia went with the young man into the woods. He was kind and friendly, and told her many things about the birds. She wasn't afraid of him anymore. Perhaps in her heart a dream of love was born. But she couldn't understand why he killed and stuffed the birds he liked so much.

II

24   At the edge of the woods a great pine tree stood. Sylvia knew it well. That night she thought of the tree. If she climbed it early in the morning, she could see the whole world. Couldn't she watch the heron fly, and find its hidden nest? What an adventure it would be! And how happy her friend would be! The young man and the old woman slept well that night, but Sylvia thought of her adventure. She forgot to think of sleep. At last, when the night birds stopped singing, she quietly left the house.

25   There was the tall pine tree, still asleep in the moonlight. First she climbed a smaller tree next to it. Then she made the dangerous step across to the old pine. The birds in the woods below her were waking up. She must climb faster if she wanted to see the heron as it left its nest. The tree seemed to grow taller as she went up. The pine tree must have been surprised to feel this small person climbing up. It must have loved this new animal in its arms. Perhaps it moved its branches a little, to help her climb. Sylvia's face shone like a star when she reached the top. She was tired, but very happy. She could see ships out to sea. Woods and farms lay for miles and miles around her. The birds sang louder and louder. At last the sun came up. Where was the

heron's nest? Look, look, Sylvia! A white spot rises up from the green trees below. The spot grows larger. The heron flies close. A wild, light bird, wide wings, and a long thin neck. He stops in the tree beyond Sylvia. Wait, wait, Sylvia! Do not move a foot or a finger, to frighten it away!

26   A moment later, Sylvia sighs. A large company of noisy birds comes to the tree, and the heron goes away. It flies down to its home in the green world below. Sylvia knows its secret now. She climbs back down. Now she is almost crying. Her fingers hurt, and her feet slip. She wonders what the young man will say to her. What will he think when she tells him how to find the heron's nest?

27   "Sylvy, Sylvy," her grandmother called, but nobody answered.

28   The young man woke up and dressed. He wanted to begin hunting again. He was sure Sylvia knew something about the white heron. Here she comes now. Her small face is white, her old dress is torn and dirty. The grandmother and the young man wait at the door to question her. The time has come to tell about the heron's nest.

29   But Sylvia does not speak. The young man looks into her eyes. He will make them rich. She wants to make him happy. He waits to hear the story she can tell.

30   No, she must keep silent! What is it that keeps her quiet? This is the first time the world has put out a hand to her. Does she have to push it away because of a bird? She hears again the wind blowing in the pine tree. She remembers how the white heron flew through the golden air. She remembers how they watched the sea and the morning together. Sylvia cannot speak. She cannot tell the heron's secret and give its life away.

31   Poor Sylvia! She was sad when the young man went away. She could have helped him. She would have followed him like a dog. She would have loved him as a dog loves! Many nights afterwards Sylvia remembered his "Halloa" as she came home with the cow. She forgot the sharp sound of his gun. She forgot the birds, wet with blood. Were the birds better friends than the hunter? Who can tell?

32   Oh, Woods! Oh, Summertime! Remember what riches were lost to her. Bring her your riches instead, your beauties and your gifts. Tell all your secrets to this lonely country child!

AFTER YOU READ THE STORY

A. Understanding the Main Ideas

Answer these questions with complete sentences.

1. At the beginning of the story, why was Sylvia afraid of the young man?
2. How did the grandmother act with the young man?
3. Why was the young man killing birds?
4. Why did he say he would pay ten dollars?
5. Why did he think Sylvia could help him?
6. Why did she watch the toad so carefully?
7. Why did she leave the house before the sun came up?
8. Why did she climb the tall pine tree?
9. What was the heron's secret?
10. Why couldn't she give away the heron's secret?

B. Close Reading

Complete the sentences below by choosing **a, b,** or **c.** The first part of the sentence tells you something that happened in the story. The second part tells you when it happened.

1. Sylvia went to bring home the cow
   a. when the cow was ready to eat.
   b. just as it began to get dark.
   c. just after her grandmother was ready to eat.

2. Sylvia began to feel frightened
   a. at the same time that she heard the young man call out.
   b. after it began to get dark.
   c. when she lost the cow.

3. The young man wanted to stay with Sylvia and her grandmother
   a. before they ate dinner.
   b. while it began to get dark, but not after.
   c. during the time that he hunted for birds.

4. They sat in the doorway
   a. as the moon came up.
   b. before it began to get dark.
   c. while the birds sang softly.

5. Sylvia decided to find the heron's nest
   a. as she was watching the toad.
   b. before it was dark.
   c. sometime during the night.

6. She had to climb the pine tree
   a. after the young man woke up.
   b. while it began to get dark.
   c. shortly before the sun came up.

7. She decided not to tell the young man where the heron lived
   a. before he said he would pay ten dollars.
   b. just as it began to get dark.
   c. after she saw how beautiful the heron was.

C. Discussion

1. What do you think about the kind of hunting the young man is doing in this story? Is it work? play? sport? science? The story was written about 100 years ago. Would you feel differently about him if he were hunting today? Why, or why not?
2. As you were reading the story, what did you think Sylvia would do? Do you think she should have helped the young man? Why, or why not?
3. The story says that Sylvia "couldn't understand why he killed the birds he liked so much." Explain her feelings for the birds, compared to the feelings of the young man. The young man tells her grandmother, "I stuff them to save them." In what way does he "save" the birds? How do we try to save birds (or other animals) today?

D. Vocabulary Practice

Match the phrase in column A to the sentence with the same meaning in column B. Then write a new sentence, using the column A word or phrase in place of the underlined phrase.

Example:

A	B
getting darker	The woods were already <u>filled with shadows</u>.

The woods were already getting darker.

A	B
quite far away	1. She knows <u>every foot of</u> the woods.
faithfully	2. Sylvy, <u>step round</u> and set a plate for the gentleman.
lowered	3. You might <u>do better</u> if you went out to the road.
happily	4. This is the first time the world has <u>put out its hand to</u> her.
hurry up	5. The road is <u>a good ways</u> from here.
a lot about	6. Sylvia's face shone <u>like a star</u>.
have more success	7. She <u>dropped</u> her head like a broken flower.
tried to help	8. From the top of the tree Sylvia could see <u>the whole world</u>.
for miles	9. She would have loved him <u>as a dog loves</u>.

Write the new sentences here.

1. _____

2. _____

3. _____

4. _____

5. _____

6. _____

7. _____

_____

8. _____

_____

9. _____

_____

E. Word Forms

From the chart below, choose the form of the word that best fits the sentences below.

Noun	Verb	Adjective	Adverb
surprise	surprise	surprising	surprisingly
secret	secrete	secretive	secretly
hunter	hunt	hunted	
shadow	shadow	shadowy	
comfort	comfort	comfortable	comfortably
stuffing	stuff	stuffed	

1. (*surprise*) By the second day of his visit, Sylvia was
   _____ friendly with the young man.

2. (*secret*) Sylvia was a _____ child, perhaps because
   she was alone so much of the time.

3. (*hunt*) The young man was an unusual kind of
   _____.

4. (*shadow*) Neither Sylvia nor the cow was afraid of the
   _____ darkness. They were used to the woods.

5. (*comfort*) The three new-made friends were _____
   with one another.

6. (*stuff*) What kind of _____ did the young man use
   inside his birds?

F. Language Activity: A Class Project on Animal Services

For this exercise, work in pairs or small groups. Work on Option I or Option II.

Option I (If you live in a place with English language public services.)

In the business or commercial pages (Yellow Pages) of a telephone book, find the name of an organization or public service that helps animals. You will find these names by looking under words or titles like these: *Animal Hospitals; Animal Organizations; Animal Shelters; Environmental, Conservation, and Ecology Organizations;* or *Environmental and Ecological Services.* Choose *one* organization or service to study. Your job is to find information about it and report that information to the class. Find the information you need in one of the following ways:

1. Telephone. Find the telephone number of the organization or service in the Yellow Pages. Some organizations and services give recorded information over the telephone. At others, you will speak to a person who can give you information.
2. A visit. The Yellow Pages usually lists the street address of the organization. If it is near you, visit the offices of the organization. Talk to the people there. Ask if they have some printed information that you can take away with you.
3. A letter. Write a letter to the organization or service asking it to send you information. Use the following form for your letter:

Your name
Your address
Date (month, day, year)

Name of Organization or Service
Address of Organization or Service

Dear Sir or Madam:

(write your request for information)

Sincerely yours,
  (sign your name here)

Your Name

Option II (If you do not live in a place with Engish language public services.)

Read Option I, above, to understand the idea behind this exercise. Then find the name of an animal services organization anywhere in the world that uses English as its first language. (Use the Internet, a local English-language consulate or embassy, or a library, or ask your teacher.) Then write a letter to the organization, as in item 3, above.

G. Writing: A Story

Write a narrative (story) of your own. Choose one of these suggestions.

1. You are Sylvia. You have told the young man where to find the heron. You go with him to hunt the bird. What happened then? How did you feel about it? What did you do?
2. You are the young man. When you see that Sylvia won't tell you where to find the bird, you try to persuade her to tell you. What happened then? Did she finally tell you? What did you do? How did you feel?
3. You are the grandmother. The day after the hunter left, you found Sylvia in tears. Years later, you tell the story of what happened to Sylvia. Did she remain sad, or become happy again? Why? What became of her when she got older?

8

OF THE COMING
OF JOHN

Adapted from the story by

W. E. B. DU BOIS

W. E. B. Du Bois (pronounced Do-BOYS) was born in 1868 in Great Barrington, Massachusetts. He was the only black student in his class at school. He was an excellent student and began to write for a black newspaper when he was fifteen. He went to Fisk University, a college for black students in Nashville, Tennessee. He later wrote that those first years in the South were difficult for him. He felt that it was even harder in the South than in the North for black people to live in a world where whites had all the power. Du Bois later studied at the University of Berlin in Germany, and he was the first African American to earn a Ph.D. from Harvard University. Later he taught at Atlanta University, and also lived and worked in New York City. Du Bois became an important leader in the fight for black equality in the United States. He helped begin the NAACP (National Association for the Advancement of Colored People) and for many years, he managed its magazine, *The Crisis*. Du Bois believed strongly that civil rights (equality under the law) were even more important than jobs and that blacks should try for the highest education. When he was ninety-three, he decided he could live no longer in the United States where he had found it impossible to turn his beliefs into reality. He moved to Ghana, in Africa, in 1961, and died two years later. "Of the Coming of John" is from his most famous book, *The Souls of Black Folk* (1903).

BEFORE YOU READ THE STORY

A. About the Author

Read the paragraph about W. E. B. Du Bois on page 97. How would you describe the main subject of his life and work?

B. Scanning for Information

W. E. B. Du Bois lived in many different places during his long life. Search the paragraph about him on page 97 in order to find *where* Du Bois did different things in his life. The first one is done for you. Try to complete the exercise in less than two minutes.

1. was born   *Great Barrington, Massachusetts*

2. went to college   _____

3. earned a Ph.D.   _____

4. taught   _____

5. lived and worked   _____

6. died   _____

C. The Pictures

1. Look at the two groups of people in the picture on page 101. What are the differences in their color, and the look on their faces? What do you think is happening?
2. On page 104, two men and a woman are seated in a music hall. Look at their faces. What do you think each one is feeling? What might happen next?

D. Thinking About It

At the time of this story, laws in the United States separated white people from black people in the way they lived their daily lives. More of these laws existed in the southern states than in the northern states. In the South, neighborhoods, schools, churches, tables in restaurants, waiting rooms and bathrooms in public places, seats on trains or buses were all separate for blacks and whites. In this story, the phrase used to describe this separation is "the color line." In 1954, a court decision made separate schools against national law. Do you believe that a color line still exists in the United States, today? If so, what forms does it take?

ghost   *Ghost* often means the part of a person that continues to exist and appear to others after the person has died. In this story *ghost* means (a) someone who doesn't seem real to others, or (b) a spirit or feeling that frightens you because it will not go away and leave you alone.

judge   A *judge* is the man or woman who manages a court of law. It is an important job in all countries. In the United States, *Judge* is often used as part of a judge's name: We say Judge Smith or the Judge, instead of Mr., Mrs., or Ms. Smith.

proud   Usually, we are *proud* of ourselves when we do something well. We are *proud* of people we know when they do good things that make us feel good, too.

respect, respectful   We *respect* a person who we think is important, perhaps more important than we are. We are *respectful* of these people, we look up to them, because of their power or importance or beauty or money or goodness.

spoil, spoiled   The simplest meaning of *spoil (spoiled)* is "destroy (destroyed)." Food that is *spoiled* is no longer good to eat, and it may make you sick. If we say that a child is *spoiled*, we mean that the child has been given too much and now knows how to take, but not how to give. When we worry that an experience or event could *spoil* a person we love, we worry that he or she might be hurt or made worse in some way.

OF THE COMING OF JOHN

I

The bell rings at Wells Institute, and the students come in for supper. Tall and black, they move slowly, like ghosts against the light of sunset. Perhaps they *are* ghosts here. For this is a college for black students outside of a white city. The students almost never go into the city. The students almost don't exist for the whites.

2   Every evening, there is one student who always runs in late. The other students laugh as John hurries in after the bell. At first, his teachers excuse his lateness. He is a tall, thin brown boy. He seems to be growing out of his clothes.

He is young and thoughtless. But he has a nice smile. He seems happy with the world.

3   John Jones came to Wells Institute from Altamaha in southeast Georgia. The white people of Altamaha thought John was a good boy. He was a good farm worker. And he was always smiling and respectful. But they shook their heads in wonder when his mother sent him north to college. The white mailman said what most of the white people thought. "It will spoil him—destroy him," he said seriously. And he spoke as if he knew.

4   But on the day John left for college, half the black folk in town followed him to the train. They were so proud of him. The girls kissed him goodbye. The boys laughed and shook his hand. The train whistled. It was time to go. He kissed his little sister. He threw his long arms around his mother. The train whistled again, and carried him north, through the fields and farms, to Wells Institute.

5   John was their friend, brother, and son. After he left, his people kept saying proudly, "When John comes . . ." So many things would happen when John came home. Parties, speaking in church. John would learn to be a teacher, and there would be a new schoolhouse. They had so many hopes for how John would help them. "When John comes . . ." But the white people wondered. They shook their heads. "School will spoil him."

6   At first, John was going to come home at Christmas. But the vacation was too short. Then for the summer. But his mother was poor, and the school cost a lot. So he worked at the Institute instead. Time went by, and two years passed. John's friends grew up, and his mother grew gray. His little sister, Jennie, went to work in a white man's kitchen. This man was a judge, rich and important.

7   Up at the Judge's house, the white people liked to hear the blacks say, "When John comes . . ." The Judge and his wife had a son named John, too. Their son John was tall and blond. When they were little, the two Johns had sometimes played together. Now he was away at college, too. At Princeton University. His parents were very proud of him. "He'll show those Northerners what a Southern gentleman can do!" the Judge would say proudly. And then he would say to Jennie, "How's *your* John? Too bad your mother sent

him away to school. It will spoil him." He shook his head. Jennie listened to him respectfully. And she wondered.

II

8   Up at Wells Institute, John's teachers were seriously worried about him. He was loud and noisy, always laughing and singing. He didn't know how to study. He seemed bored by books, and his schoolwork was careless. He was always late for everything. One night his teachers met together to discuss him. They decided "that John Jones, because of continual lateness and careless work, must leave Wells Institute." Now John understood for the first time that school was really important. He understood at last that his noise and carelessness and continual lateness had got him into serious trouble with his teachers.

9   "But don't tell Mammy—you won't write to my mother, will you?" he said. "If you don't tell her, I'll go into the city and work. And I'll come back next fall and show you something." His teachers liked him. They wanted to help him. They agreed that he could come back in the fall and try again.

10   It seemed to his teachers that John's face was always serious after that. When he returned to the Institute he began to respect his education, and he worked hard. He grew in body as well as mind. Slowly his clothes began to fit him better. His shirts were clean and his shoes were shiny. As the days passed he became more thoughtful. His teachers began to see that this careless boy was becoming a serious man.

11   Now John began to look at the world around him. He began to notice the difference between the lives of blacks and whites. He became angry when whites spoke to him without respect. Because he felt like a ghost in their world, he spent long hours worrying about the color line.

12   At last the day came when John finished Wells Institute. It was time to go back to Altamaha. He had always planned to work there after college. But now he wondered about living in that small town. Altamaha was deep in the South. Life wasn't easy for colored folk in the North, but it was even harder in the South. John knew he had to go back home. But he needed to take some time for himself first. So he decided to visit New York City first. "A breath of northern air before I go down South," he told himself.

III

13   It was a bright morning in September. John sat watching the people walk by on the New York streets. He looked at all the rich clothes, the fashionable hats. "This is the big world, the *real* world," he thought.

14   He saw a lot of people going into a grand building. He was interested, and wondered what they were going to see. When he saw a tall blond man and a fashionably dressed woman go inside, he decided to follow.

15   Inside, John found himself in a line to buy tickets. He wasn't sure what to do. He had very little money. But he pulled out a five-dollar bill he had carefully saved. He was very surprised when he got no change back. How could he spend so much money on—what?

16   John began to hear soft voices behind him. "Be careful," he heard a woman say. She seemed to be joking with the man beside her. "You mustn't get angry just because a black man is in front of you in line."

17   "You don't understand us Southerners," said the blond man beside her. "You say there's no color line in the North. But we're more friendly to colored folk than you are. Why, my best friend when I was a boy was black. He was named John after me. We're friendly, but we don't spoil them, there."

18   They all sat down in the large music hall. In front of them, musicians and singers were ready to begin. The blond man looked angry when he saw that John was sitting beside them. But John didn't notice. He was too busy looking around. The inside of the building was beautiful. This was a world so different from his! Then the singing began. John felt that he was in a dream. He closed his eyes. The beautiful music rose up in the air. He wanted so much to rise up with it. He wanted to leave his low life. To fly like a bird in the free, sweet air. To live with pride in a world of beauty, and to feel that others respected him. As John sat forward to listen, his arm touched the lady next to him. The blond man noticed, and his face grew red. He lifted his arm to call someone.

19   John was completely lost in the music. At first he didn't hear the usher.

20   "Please come with me, sir," the usher said softly. John was surprised. As he stood up, he saw the angry face of the blond man for the first time. The man recognized John. And John saw that the man was the Judge's son.

21   "I'm sorry sir," the usher said when they had left the music hall. "We gave you the wrong seat. That seat was already sold. I am so sorry. Of course, we will give you back your money . . ."

22   But John turned and walked out of the building. "You're such a fool, John," he said, now angry at himself. He walked to his hotel and wrote a letter. "Dear mother and sister—I am coming—John."

IV

23   Down in Altamaha, all the world knew John was coming. Most of the black folk came to meet his train. They were proud and excited. "John's coming!" they called to each other. They talked about the party for John at the church that night. They laughed and listened for the whistle of the train.

24   But John felt unhappy as he got off the train and looked around him. He was already angry because he had to ride south in a train car for blacks only. Now, the small, dirty town, the colorful, dirty faces of his people, made him sad. He had little to say to the happy group who came to welcome him. And the people quickly began to wonder about him. Was this cold, silent man their John? They had waited so long for him to come. Where was his smile, his laughter, his friendly handshake?

25   "He seems rather serious," said the minister of the church. "Or too proud for us?" his neighbor wondered. But the white mailman, passing by, said, "That fool black boy went north and got full of foolish ideas. But they won't work in Altamaha." The other whites agreed.

26   The welcome-home party at the church that night was a failure. Rain spoiled the barbeque. The ice cream melted. John was still cold and silent, and people didn't understand what was wrong. Then it was time for John to speak. He told his people that the world was changing. He spoke about the need for blacks to work to change the color line. More schools were needed, and better jobs. Blacks needed to forget their differences. They needed to work together to make better lives.

27   When he finished, the church was silent. People looked at each other in surprise. They didn't understand John. He

had changed. He was not the boy they had known. He had become different from them.

28   John walked quietly out of the church. He stood alone in the darkness. His sister Jennie followed him.

29   "John," she said softly, "does it make everyone unhappy when they study and learn lots of things?"

30   He smiled at her. "I'm afraid it does," he said.

31   "And John, are you glad you studied?"

32   "Yes," he answered slowly. But he sounded sure of himself.

33   Jennie said thoughtfully, "I wish I was unhappy, John. And—and—I think I *am* a little unhappy." She put her arms around him.

34   A few days later, John went up to the Judge's house. He wanted to ask if he could become the teacher at the school for black children.

35   The Judge met him at the front door. "Go around to the back door and wait, John," he said. His face was unfriendly.

36   John sat on the kitchen stairs and waited. "I keep making mistakes," he said to himself. "Everything I do is wrong. I came home to help my people. But even before I left the train station, I hurt their feelings. I wanted to teach them what I think about the color line, and they don't understand. I told myself to show respect to the Judge. But then I go to his front door. I should know better!"

37   Just then Jennie opened the kitchen door. She said the Judge would see him now. When he went in, the Judge didn't ask him to sit down. Right away, he said, "You want to teach school, I suppose. Well, John, I want to tell you something. You know I am a friend of your people. I've helped your family. I would have helped you more if you hadn't gone away North. Now, I like you colored people. But you and I both know that in this country black people can't be equal to whites. You can be good and respectful workers. And I will try to help you. But the question is—will you teach your people to be good workers, like their mothers and fathers are? I knew your father, John. He belonged to my brother. He was a good black. Will you be like him? Or will you try to put foolish ideas in people's heads? Will you spoil them by making them think they are equal to whites?"

38   "I know how things are here," John quickly answered. But the Judge looked at him, and wondered.

V

39   A month after John opened the school for black children, the Judge's son came home. This other John was tall and blond and sure of himself. His family was so proud of him. The whole white town was glad to see him come home. But things did not go well between John and his father. The Judge wanted his son to stay in Altamaha. He hoped his son would be a leader in town, like himself. But John thought the town was small and uninteresting—very boring, in fact. "Nothing here but dirt and blacks," he would say. "What could be more boring than that?" And he and the Judge would argue about it.

40   One evening when they were arguing about John's future, the mailman came to visit.

41   "I hear John's getting everybody excited over at the black school," he said.

42   "What do you mean?" asked the Judge.

43   "Oh, nothing much. Just, he talks to them about respect, and equality. About not saying 'sir' to a white man. Things like that."

44   "Who is this John?" asked the Judge's son.

45   "Why, it's little black John. You used to play with him," answered the Judge.

46   John looked angry, but then he laughed. "Oh," he said, "I saw him in New York. That's the black man that tried to push in and sit next to the lady I was with. . . ."

47   But the Judge had heard enough. All day, he had been feeling angry with his own John. Now it was time to do something about the other John. He went right to the school house door.

48   "John!" the Judge called out. His face was red with anger. "This school is closed. You children, go home and get to work. The white people of Altamaha are not spending their money on colored people just to fill their heads with foolish ideas! Go home! I'll close the door myself!"

49   Back at the Judge's house, his son looked around for something to do. He was bored with everything. His father's books were old, the town newspaper was foolish. He tried to sleep, but it was too hot. Finally, he walked out into the fields. "I feel like I'm in prison," he thought to himself. John wasn't really a bad young man. Just a little spoiled. And he

was so sure of himself, like his proud father. "There isn't even a pretty girl around here," he said angrily.

50   Just then, he saw Jennie coming down the road. "I never noticed what a pretty girl she is!" he said to himself. "Hello, Jennie," he called out to her. "You haven't even given me a kiss since I came home!"

51   Jennie looked at him with surprise. She smiled respectfully and tried to pass by. But John was bored, and felt like playing with her. He took her arm. She was afraid, and turned and ran away. John ran after her.

52   Jennie's brother John was coming down the road. His heart was sad, and his thoughts were angry. "I can't live here anymore," he was thinking. "I'll go north and find work. I'll bring Mother and Jennie with me." He had never been so unhappy.

53   Suddenly he saw his sister in front of him. He heard her cry out in fear. John could see she was trying to escape from the arms of the tall, blond man. Without thinking, John picked up a tree branch. He hit the Judge's son hard, on the head. The young man fell down. His face was covered with blood.

54   John walked slowly home. "Mammy, I'm going away," he said. "I'm going to be free."

55   "Are you going North, son? Are you going North again?"

56   "Yes, Mammy, I'm going . . . North."

57   John walked slowly back down the road to wait for the white men. He saw blood on the ground where John's white body had fallen. They had played together as boys. He wondered where those little boys had gone. He thought about his life in the North. He seemed to hear again the singing from the beautiful music hall. Listen! But maybe it was only the men coming to get him. As he waited and listened, the sound became louder and louder, like a storm coming. He saw the old Judge, leading the other men. His face was white, his eyes red with anger. John felt sorry for him—so sorry. Then the men reached him, and the storm broke all around him.

58   And the world whistled in his ears.

AFTER YOU READ THE STORY

A. Understanding the Main Ideas

Answer the following questions with complete sentences. The questions follow the f ive parts, I–V, of the story.

Part I
1. In what way were the students at Wells Institute "like ghosts"? (paragraph 1)
2. What did the white people think about John going north to college? (paragraph 5)

Part II
3. Why do John's teachers tell him that he must leave the Institute? What is he like when he returns to college? (paragraphs 8 and 10)

Part III
4. What does the usher say to John about leaving his seat? Is it true? Why did the usher speak to John at all? (paragraphs 18–21)

Part IV
5. Is the Judge happy that John wants to teach in the school for black children? Why, or why not? (paragraphs 35–38)

Part V
6. Why does John say to his mother, "Yes, Mammy, I'm going . . . North"? (paragraph 56)

B. Close Reading

In these sentences, characters in the story are wondering about something. For each sentence, choose the ending that best explains *what* they are wondering or *why* they are wondering it.

1. (paragraph 3) *"But they shook their heads in wonder when his mother sent him north to college,"* because
   a. John was a very bad student.
   b. the college was for black students only.
   c. they thought college would spoil him.

2. (paragraph 7) "*Jennie listened to him respectfully. And she wondered.*" She wondered
   a. why college was good for the Judge's John but not *her* John.
   b. if she was doing a good enough job in the Judge's house.
   c. if the Judge thought she should go to Princeton University.

3. (paragraph 12) "*But now he wondered about living in that small town,*" because
   a. he didn't think he could find work there.
   b. he believed that the color line would make his life very difficult there.
   c. his college studies had taught him that small towns were not good places to live.

4. (paragraph 24) "*And the people quickly began to wonder about him,*" because
   a. they couldn't believe he had learned so much at college.
   b. they didn't understand why he had to ride to town in a train car for blacks only.
   c. they remembered a John who was happy and friendly.

5. (paragraph 38) " '*I know how things are here,*' *John quickly answered. But the Judge looked at him, and wondered.*" The Judge wondered
   a. if John had learned enough at college to be a good teacher.
   b. if John would try to put foolish ideas into the students' heads.
   c. if John's father had been "a good black."

6. (paragraph 57) "*He wondered where those little boys had gone,*" because
   a. he could find no sign anywhere now of their old happiness or goodness.
   b. he didn't understand that he had killed the Judge's son.
   c. he understood that the boys hadn't liked each other even when they were little.

C. Discussion

1. What does the final sentence of the story mean? What happens to John at the end of the story? Will life be different for the black people of Altamaha after this?
2. Do you think John's mother was right to send him away to college? Why, or why not?
3. This story was written almost 100 years ago. Think of a small town like Altamaha in your home country today. How much would you say it has changed in the past 100 years? Completely? Somewhat? Not at all? Are the changes in those small towns just like the changes in the cities, or are they different?

D. Vocabulary Practice

Complete the following sentences in a way that shows the meaning of the underlined word. In this exercise, you are asked to speak about your own ideas or experience.

1. One of the people I have great <u>respect</u> for is _____ ,

   and this is because _____

   _____ .

2. One thing I did in the past that I am <u>proud</u> of is that I _____

   _____ .

3. I believe that <u>ghosts</u> _____

   _____ .

4. When I was little, the thing that was most <u>boring</u> to me was

   _____ , and that was because _____

   _____ .

5. Am I a <u>serious</u> person? Well, I am always serious when I

   _____ , and I am never serious when I _____

   _____ .

E. Word Forms

To the left of each sentence below is the *verb* form of a word. You are asked to fill in the space in the sentence with a different form of that word. The chart below will help you find the right form. Some of the word forms below will be new words for you, so you must choose by deciding which form fits into the sentence.

Noun	Verb	Adjective	Adverb
respect	respect	respectful	respectfully
fool	fool	foolish	foolishly
bore (person), boredom (feeling)	bore	boring	boringly
failure	fail	failed, failing	
spoilage	spoil	spoiled	
judge (person), judgment (decision)	judge	judgmental	judgmentally

1. (*respect*) "I hope your son will come home soon, too," Jennie said to the Judge _____.

2. (*fool*) John thought: "So many people came to welcome me back home, but I said almost nothing to them. How could I have been such a _____?"

3. (*bore*) After he returned home, the Judge's son John felt a heavy sense of _____ all day, every day.

4. (*fail*) John's mother wanted the church party to be a great success, but instead it was a _____.

5. (*spoil*) The Judge's son was a _____ young man, but perhaps not really bad.

6. (*judge*) Who would you go to for a fair _____ in the case of John against John?

F. Language Activity: A World of Meaning

Sometimes we can tell the exact meaning of a word only by thinking about the situation that the word helps to describe. In this story, the word *world* is used a number of times to mean different things. Read again the following sentences from the story and say in your own words what *the world* means in each case.

1. (paragraph 11) "Now [after he returned to the Institute] John began to look at the world around him." This means John began to notice _____

   _____ .

2. (paragraph 13) " 'This is the big world, the *real* world,' he thought." (paragraph 18) "This was a world so different from his!" In New York, some of the things that make up this world are: _____

   _____ .

3. (paragraph 23) "Down in Altamaha, all the world knew John was coming." *The world* here means _____

   _____ .

4. (paragraph 26) "He told his people that the world was changing." John wants to tell his people that _____

   _____ .

5. (paragraph 58) "And the world whistled in his ears." Here, *the world* is _____

   _____ .

G. Writing: A Dialog

Choose *one* of the moments from the story (1, 2, or 3 below) when two people are talking to each other. Write down in your own words the rest of what you think these two people said to each other (a dialog). Write down also how they moved or what they did when they spoke, or how they spoke. With a partner or with any two other people, practice speaking the dialog you wrote. Practice until you can almost say it without looking at your paper. Then speak or read the dialog in front of the class. It will help you "become" the person in the dialog if you wear a hat or other piece of clothing that you think the person would wear. If you wish, you can use the beginnings given below. Or you can begin in your own way.

1. The Judge is talking with John's mother about her decision to send him north to college. Paragraphs 3–7 will give you some ideas for this dialog.
   Judge: So you've decided to send John to college, have you?
   John's mother: (*She looks down.*) Yes, Judge, he'll take the train tomorrow.
   Judge: (*He shakes his head.*) I think this is a bad idea, Mrs. Jones. Very bad.
   John's mother: (*She looks up.*) Why do you say that, Judge?

2. John is talking with the director of Wells Institute about how he is doing in his studies. Paragraphs 2, 6, and 8 will give you some ideas for this dialog.
   Director: (*looking very serious*) Step into my office for a moment please, John.
   John: (*nervous*) Yes, sir. Um, I'm sorry I'm late, sir.
   Director: Well, that is one thing we must talk about, John.
   John: Really, sir? (*acting surprised*) What do you mean?

3. John and his sister Jennie are talking about the changes in John and what caused these changes. Paragraphs 27–33 will give you some ideas for this dialog.
   Jennie: (*softly*) John, does it make everyone unhappy when they study and learn lots of things?
   John: (*He smiles at her.*) I'm afraid it does.
   Jennie: And John, are you glad you studied?
   John: (*slowly at first*) Yes. (*then stronger*) Yes! But now . . .

9

THE LADY, OR
THE TIGER?

Adapted from the story by
FRANK R. STOCKTON

Frank R. Stockton was born in 1834. His most famous stories are in
the form of fairy tales, ghost stories, or romances. But in all of them
his humor has an edge like a knife. When "The Lady, or the Tiger?"
appeared in *Century Magazine* in 1882, it caused excitement all over
the country. Hundreds of people wrote letters to the magazine or to
their newspapers about it. Many letters demanded an answer to the
question that the story asks. Others asked if the story was really about
government, or psychology, or the battle of the sexes, or something
else. Wisely, Stockton never answered any of the letters. The story re-
mains as fresh today as it was then. Frank Stockton died in 1902.

BEFORE YOU READ THE STORY

A. About the Author

Read the paragraph about Frank Stockton on page 115. In what magazine was this story first published? How did the readers respond to Stockton's story?

B. The Pictures

1. Look at the picture on page 118. Judging from their clothes, what kind of people are they? When did they live?
2. The title of the story asks a question. Think about what question it is asking. Now look at the picture on page 122. What does the picture show? Where is the man going? What might he be looking at?

C. Thinking About It

A phrase you will read early in the story is "the first law of Chance." This phrase suggests that chance, or luck, follows certain laws, or rules. Do you agree? Which is more important to you in your life: laws and rules, or chance and luck? Why do you think so?

D. Scanning

Sometimes we have to scan quickly an entire book, or sections of a book, for information. In this exercise, you will scan the biographies of all the writers in *Great American Stories 1*.

First, read these questions. Then scan the biographies of the writers to find the answers. Try to do the entire exercise in no more than five minutes.

1. Which writers wrote mostly in the nineteenth century? Which wrote mostly in the twentieth century?
2. Which writers died in the twentieth century?
3. List which ones were men. List which ones were women.
4. Which writers traveled outside the United States for long periods of time?
5. Which writers were known for their stories about special areas of the United States?

semi-barbaric   This story begins: "A long, long time ago, there was a *semi-barbaric* king." *Semi-* means "partly," "somewhat," "about half." *Barbaric* means "not following the usual rules of polite behavior." In this story, the *semi-barbaric* king makes his own laws, and loves making his own laws.

imagination   *Imagination* is the power we have to make pictures in our mind of things that are not present. We can use that power in our work, or we can use it to dream of new ideas or things.

jealous   In this story, a father is *jealous* of his daughter. This means he wants to control her, especially her relations with young men. And the daughter is *jealous* of the young man she loves. She wants him for herself alone; she doesn't want to share him with anyone else.

THE LADY, OR THE TIGER?

A long, long time ago, there was a semi-barbaric king. I call him semi-barbaric because the modern world, with its modern ideas, had softened his barbarism a little. But still, his ideas were large, wild, and free. He had a wonderful imagination. He was also a king of the greatest powers, and he easily turned the dreams of his imagination into facts. He greatly enjoyed talking to himself about ideas. And, when he and himself agreed upon a thing, the thing was done. He was a very pleasant man when everything in his world moved smoothly. And when something went wrong, he became even more pleasant. Nothing, you see, pleased him more than making wrong things right.

2   One of this semi-barbaric king's modern ideas was the idea of a large arena. In this arena, his people could watch both men and animals in acts of bravery.

3   But even this modern idea was touched by the king's wild imagination. In his arena, the people saw more than soldiers fighting soldiers, or men fighting animals. They enjoyed more than the sight of blood. In the king's arena, the

people saw the laws of the country at work. They saw good men lifted up and bad men pushed down. Most important, they were able to watch the workings of the First Law of Chance.

4   Here is what happened when a man was accused of a crime. If the king was interested in the crime, then the people were told to come to the arena. They came together and sat there, thousands of them. The king sat high up in his king's chair. When he gave a sign, a door below him opened. The accused man stepped out into the arena. Across from him, on the other side of the arena, were two other doors. They were close together and they looked the same. The accused man would walk straight to these doors and open one of them. He could choose either one of the doors. He was forced by nothing and led by no one. Only Chance helped him—or didn't help him.

5   Behind one of the doors was a tiger. It was the wildest, biggest, hungriest tiger that could be found. Of course, it quickly jumped on the man. The man quickly—or not so quickly—died. After he died, sad bells rang, women cried, and the thousands of people walked home slowly.

6   But, if the accused man opened the other door, a lady would step out. She was the finest and most beautiful lady that could be found. At that moment, there in the arena, she would be married to the man. It didn't matter if the man was already married. It didn't matter if he was in love with another woman. The king did not let little things like that get in the way of his imagination. No, the two were married there in front of the king. There was music and dancing. Then happy bells rang, women cried, and the thousands of people walked home singing.

7   This was the way the law worked in the king's semi-barbaric country. Its fairness is clear. The criminal could not know which door the lady was behind. He opened either door as he wanted. At the moment he opened the door, he did not know if he was going to be eaten or married.

8   The people of the country thought the law was a good one. They went to the arena with great interest. They never knew if they would see a bloody killing or a lovely marriage. This uncertainty gave the day its fine and unusual taste. And they liked the fairness of the law. Wasn't it true that the accused man held his life in his own hands?

The Lady, or the Tiger? **119**

9   This semi-barbaric king had a daughter. The princess was as beautiful as any flower in the king's imagination. She had a mind as wild and free as the king's. She had a heart like a volcano. The king loved her deeply, watched her closely, and was very jealous of her. But he could not always watch her. And in his castle lived a young man. This young man was a worker. He was a good worker, but he was of low birth. He was brave and handsome, and the princess loved him, and was jealous of him. Because of the girl's semi-barbarism, her love was hot and strong. Of course, the young man quickly returned it. The lovers were happy together for many months. But one day the king discovered their love. Of course he did not lose a minute. He threw the young man into prison and named a day for his appearance in the arena.

10   There had never been a day as important as that one. The country was searched for the strongest, biggest, most dangerous tiger. With equal care, the country was searched for the finest and most beautiful young woman. There was no question, of course, that the young man had loved the princess. He knew it, she knew it, the king knew it, and everybody else knew it, too. But the king didn't let this stand in the way of his excellent law. Also, the king knew that the young man would now disappear from his daughter's life. He would disappear with the other beautiful lady. Or he would disappear into the hungry tiger. The only question was, "Which?"

11   And so the day arrived. Thousands and thousands of people came to the arena. The king was in his place, across from those two doors that seemed alike but were truly very different.

12   All was ready. The sign was given. The door below the king opened, and the lover of the princess walked into the arena. Tall, handsome, fair, he seemed like a prince. The people had not known that such a fine young man had lived among them. Was it any wonder that the princess had loved him?

13   The young man came forward into the arena, and then turned toward the king's chair. But his eyes were not on the king. They were on the princess, who sat to her father's right. Perhaps it was wrong for the young lady to be there. But remember that she was still semi-barbaric. Her wild

heart would not let her be away from her lover on this day. More important, she now knew the secret of the doors. Over the past few days, she had used all of her power in the castle, and much of her gold. She had discovered which door hid the tiger, and which door hid the lady.

14   She knew more than this. She knew the lady. It was one of the fairest and loveliest ladies in the castle. In fact, this lady was more than fair and lovely. She was thoughtful, kind, loving, full of laughter, and quick of mind. The princess hated her. She had seen, or imagined she had seen, the lady looking at the young man. She thought these looks had been noticed and even returned. Once or twice she had seen them talking together. Perhaps they had talked for only a moment. Perhaps they had talked of nothing important. But how could the princess be sure of that? The other girl was lovely and kind, yes. But she had lifted her eyes to the lover of the princess. And so, in her semi-barbaric heart, the princess was jealous, and hated her.

15   Now, in the arena, her lover turned and looked at her. His eyes met hers, and he saw at once that she knew the secret of the doors. He had been sure that she would know it. He understood her heart. He had known that she would try to learn this thing which no one else knew—not even the king. He had known she would try. And now, as he looked at her, he saw that she had succeeded.

16   At that moment, his quick and worried look asked the question: "Which?" This question in his eyes was as clear to the princess as spoken words. There was no time to lose. The question had been asked in a second. It must be answered in a second.

17   Her right arm rested on the arm of her chair. She lifted her hand and made a quick movement towards the right. No one saw except her lover. Every eye except his was on the man in the arena.

18   He turned and walked quickly across the empty space. Every heart stopped beating. Every breath was held. Every eye was fixed upon that man. Without stopping for even a second, he went to the door on the right and opened it.

19   Now, the question is this: Did the tiger come out of that door, or did the lady?

20   As we think deeply about this question, it becomes harder and harder to answer. We must know the heart of the

animal called man. And the heart is difficult to know. Think of it, dear reader, and remember that the decision is not yours. The decision belongs to that hot-blooded, semi-barbaric princess. Her heart was at a white heat beneath the fires of jealousy and painful sadness. She had lost him, but who should have him?

21   Very often, in her thoughts and in her dreams, she had cried out in fear. She had imagined her lover as he opened the door to the hungry tiger.

22   And even more often she had seen him at the other door! She had bitten her tongue and pulled her hair. She had hated his happiness when he opened the door to the lady. Her heart burned with pain and hatred when she imagined the scene: He goes quickly to meet the woman. He leads her into the arena. His eyes shine with new life. The happy bells ring wildly. The two of them are married before her eyes. Children run around them and throw flowers. There is music, and the thousands of people dance in the streets. And

the princess's cry of sadness is lost in the sounds of happiness!

23   Wouldn't it be better for him to die at once? Couldn't he wait for her in the beautiful land of the semi-barbaric future?

24   But the tiger, those cries of pain, that blood!

25   Her decision had been shown in a second. But it had been made after days and nights of deep and painful thought. She had known she would be asked. She had decided what to answer. She had moved her hand to the right.

26   The question of her decision is not an easy one to think about. Certainly I am not the one person who should have to answer it. So I leave it with all of you: Which came out of the opened door—the lady, or the tiger?

AFTER YOU READ THE STORY

A. Understanding the Main Ideas

If the sentence is true, write **T** next to it. If it is not true, write **F** for false. Then rewrite the sentence so that it is true.

_____ **1.** The king and the princess were civilized people.

_____ **2.** The king believed that questions of right and wrong should be decided by Chance.

_____ **3.** There were three doors in the arena. Behind one stood the king, behind the second stood the princess, and behind the third stood the tiger.

_____ **4.** The people of the land thought the king was fair.

_____ **5.** The king was pleased that the princess and the young man were in love. He wanted them to be married in the arena.

_____ **6.** The princess was very upset because she couldn't help her lover choose the right door.

_____ **7.** The young man thought that he knew which door to choose.

B. Close Reading

In the following sentences, the words *this, that,* and *it* have been underlined. Find the sentence in the story (paragraph numbers are given to help you). Then tell what words or ideas are meant by *this, that,* or *it*.

Examples:

"Of course, the young man quickly returned it." (paragraph 9)

It means the princess's love.

"She knew more than this." (paragraph 14)

This means which door hid the tiger and which door hid the lady.

1. *"The king did not let little things like that get in the way of his imagination."* (paragraph 6)
2. *"This was the way the law worked in the king's semi-barbaric country."* (paragraph 7)
3. *This uncertainty gave the day its fine and unusual taste.* (paragraph 8)
4. *"But the king didn't let this stand in the way of his excellent law."* (paragraph 10)
5. *"But how could the princess be sure of that?"* (paragraph 14)
6. *"He had been sure that she would know it."* (paragraph 15)
7. *"Certainly I am not the one person who should have to answer it."* (paragraph 26)

C. Discussion

1. "Which came out of the opened door—the lady, or the tiger?" What do you think? Did the princess send her lover to the lady or to the tiger? Why?
2. The end of "The Lady, or the Tiger?" is about the princess's decision: whether to send her lover to the lady or to the tiger. But doesn't the lover, too, have a decision to make? Look at the picture on page 122. The lover is about to open one of the doors. In this picture, he turns and takes a final look at the princess. With a movement of her hand, she has told him to open the door on the right. This leads us to a final question. Remember, the lover knows that the princess knows which door hides the lady, and which door hides the tiger. How well does the lover know the princess? Will he

open the door she has chosen? Or, believing it hides the tiger, will he open the other one? Why, finally, did he open the door on the right?

3. Do you think people are less barbaric now than they were hundreds of years ago? In what ways? Are they more barbaric? In what ways? Are they exactly the same? Give specific examples to help others understand your thoughts.

D. Vocabulary Practice

Choose the best words from the list below to complete the sentences.

volcano	arena	imagination	Chance
accused	fair	jealous	semi-barbaric

1. The laws of that land were somewhat strange, because they were made by the _____ king.

2. People gathered in the _____ to see what would happen to the young man.

3. Only _____ helped a man decide which door to choose.

4. If someone broke a law, he was _____ of the crime. Then he had to come before the king in the arena.

5. The king had some modern ideas. But his ideas were touched by his wild _____.

6. The love in the princess's heart was as strong as a hot _____.

7. The princess felt _____ of the beautiful, gentle lady in the castle.

8. Everyone thought the working of Chance was _____ because a man's life was in his own hands.

E. Word Forms

Use the chart to help you choose the correct form of the word to put in the blank spaces in the sentences.

Noun	Verb	Adjective	Adverb
marriage	marry	married	
accusation	accuse	accused	
imagination	imagine	imaginative	imaginatively
search	search	searching	
success	succeed	successful	successfully

1. (*marriage / marry / married*) Although the princess loved the young man, the king was against their _____. If an accused man chose the door with the lady behind it, he had to _____ her. It didn't matter if he was already _____.

2. (*accusation / accuse / accused*) It was a matter of Chance whether the _____ chose the lady, or the tiger. The king _____ the young man of loving his daughter. Neither the princess nor the young man denied the _____.

3. (*imagination / imagine / imaginative*) The king was an _____ man. His laws reflected his wild _____. Can you _____ how people would feel about such a law today?

4. (*search / search / searching*) The young man gave the princess a _____ look. He was sure she must know which door hid the tiger. The princess _____ her heart to decide which door to show him. No matter which door he chose, she would have to continue her own _____ for a husband.

5. (*success / succeed / successful*) The princess _____ in giving her lover a sign. But the reader doesn't know whether the young man makes a _____ choice. And we don't know which choice would seem like a _____ to the princess.

F. Language Activity: Pair Work on Composition

With a partner, read over the instructions for the Writing exercise (Exercise G) below. Share the ideas you both have about each of the three paragraphs. Take notes as you talk. Plan each paragraph separately. Next, working alone, write the three paragraphs. Then, exchange paragraphs with your partner and discuss them. For example, are the "reasons" given in paragraphs 1 and 2 good ones? What do you think about your partner's personal choice in paragraph 3? Is it clear to you? Does it make good sense? Discuss the suggestions your partner makes for your paragraphs. Then rewrite them.

G. Writing: Three-Paragraph Composition

1. "Which came out of the opened door—the lady, or the tiger?" Write down this question. Then write a paragraph that begins with the sentence "Perhaps it was the lady who came out." Give at least three reasons why the princess chose the lady for her lover.
2. Write a second paragraph that begins "On the other hand, perhaps it was the tiger." Give at least three reasons why the princess chose the tiger.
3. Write a third paragraph that begins with the words "Personally, I think . . ." Give your own choice. Which of the reasons that you have written is the most important to you? Why?

ANSWER KEY

Answers not given will vary.

1. THE GIFT OF THE MAGI

BEFORE YOU READ THE STORY

B. Scanning for Information
1. Greensboro, North Carolina
2. Fifteen
3. He took money from a bank.
4. Stories with surprise endings
5. A book of stories about the everyday people of New York
6. 52 years old

AFTER YOU READ THE STORY

A. Understanding the Main Ideas
1. Della wanted to buy a gift for Jim because it was Christmas.
2. Della and Jim weren't rich. They had no money, and their chairs and tables were old and poor.
3. Their greatest treasures were Jim's gold watch and Della's hair.
4. She sold her hair.
5. He sold his gold watch.
6. The Magi were wise men, and they brought gifts to the baby Jesus.
7. He thinks they were wise because they loved each other so much that they gave away their greatest treasures.

B. Close Reading
1. T
2. F. Della was very sad before she bought Jim's present.
3. F. Madame Sophronie gave Della twenty dollars for her hair.
4. F. Before Christmas, Jim had a cheap chain for his watch.
5. T
6. F. Della cried when Jim gave her the combs.
7. T

D. Vocabulary Practice

1. count	3. mirror	5. comb	7. doorbell
2. treasures	4. gift	6. watch	8. wise

E. Word Forms
1. sadness, sad
2. wisdom, wise
3. happy, happiness
4. heaviness, heavy
5. expense, expensive

2. LOVE OF LIFE

BEFORE YOU READ THE STORY

A. About the Author
The Klondike is in northwest Canada, near Alaska. Men went there to find gold. It was a cold, empty place.

D. Skimming
1. two
2. his foot
3. hungry, cold, and sick
4. Men on a ship find him. He is alive.

AFTER YOU READ THE STORY

A. Understanding the Main Ideas
1. Bill was the friend of the man who hurt his foot. He thought that the man would die. He thought he would die, too, if he stopped.
2. Gold was in the bag. He kept the bag.
3. He was hungry, and the fish was food.
4. He didn't think the ship was real. He didn't believe there could be a ship in that empty place. But the ship was real.
5. The man was safe on the ship. He had enough food to eat. But he had been hungry for a long time, and he couldn't believe that he would not be hungry again.
6. The man shows that he loves life by holding onto it through many troubles.

B. Close Reading
1. b 3. a 5. b 7. a
2. c 4. c 6. c

C. Vocabulary Practice
1. strong 3. cry 5. lead 7. loudly
2. found 4. life 6. full 8. open

E. Word Forms
1. slowly, slow
2. sudden, suddenly
3. tired, tiredly
4. weak, weakly
5. hungrily, hungry

F. Language Activity: Riddles
1. d.   3. f.   5. e.   7. g.
2. c.   4. h.   6. b.   8. a.

3. THE STORY OF AN HOUR

BEFORE YOU READ THE STORY

A. About the Author

Many of Chopin's stories were about the freedom of women. Her stories were forgotten for many years, perhaps because people were still not ready to read what they said about women.

B. Scanning Two Different Sources of Information
1. Chopin   3. London   5. London
2. Chopin   4. London   6. Chopin

AFTER YOU READ THE STORY

A. Understanding the Main Ideas
1. He told her that her husband, Brently, was dead.
2. She cried loudly when she first heard the news.
3. She was waiting for something to come to her. She could not give it a name.
4. She felt joy at the thought of her new freedom.
5. Everyone was surprised because they thought Brently was dead.
6. She didn't die of joy. She died from the shock of seeing her husband and losing her new freedom.

B. Close Reading
1. weak   4. fought against   7. long
2. Brently   5. stronger   8. Louise
3. her feelings 6. alone

D. Vocabulary Practice (sample answers)
1. My aunt was very surprised when her son threw his ice cream on the floor.
2. Do you know what was really shocking about that movie? It was when the woman shot her lover. What a lot of blood! And how she laughed!
3. How did the dog show his excitement? I'll tell you. It was funny. He ran around in circles and then rolled over on his back and then ran around in circles again.
4. I felt that my heart was broken when my girlfriend ran away with my best friend in his BMW.

E. Word Forms
1. brokenly, broke, broken
2. understandingly, understand, understanding
3. joy, joyfully, joyful
4. excited, excitement, excitedly
5. freely, freedom, free

4. THE JOURNEY TO HANFORD

BEFORE YOU READ THE STORY

D. Scanning
1. Born 1908, Died 1981
2. Born and died in Fresno, California
3. *My Name Is Aram*
4. Paris

AFTER YOU READ THE STORY

A. Understanding the Main Ideas
1. F. Jorgi went to Hanford because his father and the rest of the family wanted to get him out of the way for a while.
2. T
3. T
4. F. Aram wanted to go to Hanford very much.
5. F. When Jorgi arrived in Hanford, the watermelon season was not over, but the farmer did not want Jorgi to work for him, so he told Jorgi a lie.
6. T
7. F. Aram's grandmother gave Aram money to give to his grandfather so his grandfather wouldn't know that Jorgi had brought no money home.
8. F. Aram's grandfather loved Jorgi's music. He just didn't like to say so.
9. F. Aram's rice was sometimes salty, sometimes swill, and sometimes perfect.

B. Close Reading
1. He thinks the writer is a fool for liking music. He thinks that men who play music in real life don't make any money, and therefore they are fools.
2. The writer is probably looking at a beautiful young woman who will never be his wife. The grandmother told her husband that he was no longer young, and this made him angry.

3. The grandfather thinks that that writer made few or no journeys. He thinks that only fools make journeys to new places.
4. The grandfather loves Jorgi, foolish or not. When Jorgi plays his music, the grandfather smiles in his sleep.

D. Vocabulary Practice
(In order of appearance in the paragraph:) punish, journey, zither, roar, watermelon, season, fool, praise, salty, swill, perfect

E. Word Forms

1. punishment	3. perfection	5. salt
2. praised	4. seasonal, season	6. foolish

5. THE TELL-TALE HEART

BEFORE YOU READ THE STORY

D. Skimming
Group C

AFTER YOU READ THE STORY

A. Understanding the Main Ideas

1. b	3. b	5. b
2. c	4. a	6. c

B. Close Reading

1. c	3. d	5. f	7. e
2. g	4. b	6. a	

D. Vocabulary Practice (sample answers)
1. I was sure the young man was mad when he said he could hear all things in the sky and in the earth, and when he tried to hold the lamp light on the old man's eye.
2. The thing that was most horrible for me in the story was when the young man cut up the old man's body and put the pieces under the floor boards. Ugh!
3. I felt some fear when the young man began to hear the old man's heart beating below the floor. I really felt cold down my back!
4. When he was with the police, the most dangerous thing the young man did was to begin talking louder and louder and acting more and more nervous.
5. I think the young man was nervous at the beginning of the story because he was mad, and so he was always nervous.

E. Word Forms
1. horrible, horror
2. carefully, care
3. danger, dangerous
4. nervously, nerves

F. Language Activity: Using Similes
1. b   3. c   5. a
2. a   4. b

6. TOM WHITEWASHES THE FENCE

BEFORE YOU READ THE STORY

A. About the Author
   Twain worked for a printer when he was young, and later he was a pilot, a soldier, a seeker of gold, a newspaper reporter, a novelist, and a public speaker. The name "Mark Twain" came from his work as a steamboat pilot.

D. Scanning for Numbers
1. 12 years old
2. He began writing humorous stories.
3. In 1858
4. In 1863
5. In 1866
6. 75 years old

AFTER YOU READ THE STORY

A. Understanding the Main Ideas
1. He felt sad because he had to work while all the other boys played.
2. His idea was to pretend to like the work so much that other boys would want to do it for him.
3. He had all the treasures that the other boys had given him in order to have some time with the brush. (A list of these treasures is in paragraph 35.)
4. The law is: to make a man or a boy want something, it is only necessary to make it difficult to get. He also learns that "work is whatever somebody *has* to do, and play is whatever somebody *doesn't* have to do."

B. Close Reading
1. The story takes place on a Saturday morning.
2. Tom has to whitewash the fence as a punishment for coming home late one night and climbing in through the window.

3. Jim is going to get water from the town well.
4. He paints the fence like an artist, pretending that it is not work, but an enjoyable activity.
5. Ben trades his apple for the brush.
6. Billy Fisher gives Tom a kite.

D. Vocabulary Practice
1. inviting, freedom, fence
2. brush, an artist
3. pretended, traded, brush
4. discouraged, triumph, law

E. Word Forms
1. restful, restful   3. peacefully   5. law
2. hateful   4. carefully

F. Language Activity: Colorful Language
1. b   3. c   5. b
2. a   4. b   6. a

7. A WHITE HERON

BEFORE YOU READ THE STORY

A. About the Author
Jewett writes about the simple lives of country people. Her stories take place in Maine. Most of O. Henry's stories take place in New York City.

D. Skimming
1. They are poor.
2. Sylvia knows a lot about the woods and its animals, especially the birds.
3. He wants to find, shoot, and stuff birds.
4. She likes him, but she is a little frightened by him, too.
5. Answers will vary.

AFTER YOU READ THE STORY

A. Understanding the Main Ideas
1. She was afraid because the young man was a stranger, and she didn't see many people other than her grandmother.
2. The grandmother acted in a friendly way with the young man.
3. He kills them to stuff them and save them.
4. He said he would pay ten dollars to know where the white heron's nest was.

5. Her grandmother had told him that Sylvia knew every foot of the woods and all its animals.
6. Sylvia watched the toad carefully because she didn't want the young man to see her thoughts.
7. She left the house before the sun came up in order to see the heron leave its nest.
8. She climbed the tree to get a better view of the heron.
9. The heron's secret was its nest.
10. She couldn't give away the heron's secret because then the young man would kill the beautiful bird.

B. Close Reading
1. b   3. c   5. c   7. c
2. a   4. a   6. c

D. Vocabulary Practice
1. She knows a lot about the woods.
2. Sylvy, hurry up and set a plate for the gentleman.
3. You might have more success if you went out to the road.
4. This is the first time the world has tried to help her.
5. The road is quite far away from here.
6. Sylvia's face shone happily.
7. She lowered her head like a broken flower.
8. From the top of the tree Sylvia could see for miles.
9. She would have loved him faithfully.

E. Word Forms
1. surprisingly   3. hunter   5. comfortable
2. secretive   4. shadowy   6. stuffing

8. OF THE COMING OF JOHN

BEFORE YOU READ THE STORY

A. About the Author
The main subject of his life and work was the fight for black equality and civil rights in the United States.

B. Scanning for Information
1. Great Barrington, Massachusetts
2. Fisk University in Nashville, Tennessee
3. Harvard University
4. Atlanta University
5. New York City
6. Ghana

A. Understanding the Main Ideas

1. They are like ghosts because they move slowly against the light of sunset, but also because they almost don't exist for the whites of the city.
2. They thought it would spoil him, destroy him.
3. They tell him he has to leave the Institute because he is not serious about his studies. When he returns, he is a changed person: he shows respect for his education and works hard.
4. He tells John that he was given a seat that was already sold. This was not true. The usher spoke to John because the young white man told him to.
5. He is not very happy with this idea because he is worried that John has changed and will put strange ideas into the children's heads.
6. He says this so she won't worry, but he knows that probably he is going to be killed.

B. Close Reading

1. c   3. b   5. b
2. a   4. c   6. a

E. Word Forms

1. respectfully   3. boredom   5. spoiled
2. fool   4. failure   6. judgment

F. Language Activity: A World of Meaning (sample answers)

1. the difference between the lives of blacks and whites
2. the rich clothes, fashionable hats, and grand buildings
3. everyone in town, black or white
4. blacks must work to change the color line
5. all his life till now, including the violent death now coming at him

9. THE LADY, OR THE TIGER?

BEFORE YOU READ THE STORY

A. About the Author

It was published in *Century Magazine*. Many people read this magazine, and they demanded an answer to the question asked by the story's title.

D. Scanning

1. O. Henry, Chopin, Poe, Twain, Jewett, and Stockton wrote mostly in the nineteenth century. London, Saroyan, and Du Bois wrote mostly in the twentieth century.
2. All the writers except Poe died in the twentieth century.
3. Chopin and Jewett were women, the others men.
4. London, Saroyan, Poe, Twain, and Du Bois all traveled or lived outside the United States.
5. O. Henry (New York City), Twain (Mississippi River and its towns), and Jewett (Maine).

AFTER YOU READ THE STORY

A. Understanding the Main Ideas

1. F. The king and the princess were semi-barbaric people.
2. T
3. F. There were two doors in the arena; behind one stood the lady, behind the other was the tiger.
4. T
5. F. The king was very angry because he was jealous of his daughter.
6. F. She found a way to tell him which door to open.
7. T

B. Close Reading

1. *That* means whether or not the man was married to, or in love with, another woman.
2. *This* means the accused man chooses one of two doors, and gets a lady or a tiger.
3. *This* uncertainty is not knowing whether they would see a bloody killing or a lovely marriage.
4. *This* means the fact that the young man had loved the princess, and everyone knew it.
5. *That* means the young man and the other lady had perhaps talked only for a moment and about nothing important.
6. *It* means the secret of the doors.
7. *It* means the question of the princess's decision.

D. Vocabulary Practice

1. semi-barbaric   3. Chance   5. imagination   7. jealous
2. arena   4. accused   6. volcano   8. fair

E. Word Forms
1. marriage, marry, married
2. accused, accused, accusation
3. imaginative, imagination, imagine
4. searching, searched, search
5. disappear, disappearance
6. succeeded, successful, success